HIDDEN FROM PLAIN SIGHT

...as if ordinary life mattered

Beatrice Montserrat

Copyright © Beatrice Montserrat 2023
This book is sold subject to the condition that it shall not, by way of trade or otherwise, be lent, resold, hired out, or otherwise circulated without the publisher's prior consent in any form of binding or cover other than that in which it is published and without a similar condition including this condition being imposed on the subsequent publisher.
The moral right of Beatrice Montserrat has been asserted.

CONTENTS

ACKNOWLEDGEMENTS i
INTRODUCTION 1
CHAPTER 1: THE WORKPLACE 8
CHAPTER 2: THE FAMILY 34
CHAPTER 3: FRIENDSHIPS 78
CONCLUSION 105

ACKNOWLEDGEMENTS

When thinking of thanking someone for a favour received, usually clichés come to mind which may not express fully what is meant. In the case of saying thanks for help and advice for writing a book, the usual phrase that comes to mind is: "... the author would like to thank X, Y and Z for their help, without which this book would not have been written." Another cliché, perhaps, but believe me, I now realise that it isn't. I can sincerely say that without the help of Anne Gormley this book could not have been published. I decided to ask her help because she is a recently retired secondary school teacher of English, now a tour guide, and author of a few books. Her contribution, which included checking my grammar, the content and editing, was always sincere, clear and to the point, such as: "this paragraph is weak and muddy, not clear" or "you have spelt Covid with a *t* three time on the same page", or "make sure you get rid of the older copies, I seem to have seen this before", etc. Her encouragement and practical suggestions kept me going, especially in moments when the task in hand seemed too difficult.

I also want to thank Fr. Charles Connolly who checked doctrinal issues and made very helpful suggestions.

Thanks also to Brakemi Egbedi, a student from Nigeria doing her PhD at Waterford Institute of Technology, who was not impressed when I told her the title I had originally thought of for the book. Her immediate answer was: "I would never buy a book with this title." Needless to say, I changed it.

I am also grateful to my family and friends who could not believe I was writing a book, and with their enthusiasm and prayers for its success, which helped me to forge ahead.

Many thanks to Jennifer Kehoe for her valuable contribution to the chapter on the family, where she shares her intimate experiences. I know her husband was happy with what she wrote which I am confident will be a help and encouragement to married couples.

And to those who also volunteered to share their experiences: Niamh Walsh, Gabrielle Doyle, Dr. Miriam Kennedy, Gabriela Lenze, Don Hinderer.

Thanks also to my brothers and sisters who agreed to publish the brief words about our family, especially to Josep whose poem has been included.

The topics covered in the book may prompt some to live their life – their ordinary life – in a more Christian way. I thank God for that as I also thank Him for his unmistakable intervention in all the steps towards the completion of this book.

Finally, I would like to express my sincere thanks to my publishing team at KINDLE BOOK PUBLISHING for help in publishing my book.

INTRODUCTION

When I decided to write a book, I consulted the website *The Writer*, which is addressed to those who want to write for the first time. The site gives the following advice: "As an older writer, you have a wealth of wisdom and memories to share with the world but sometimes fear can get in the way of putting yourself on the page." (How very true!)

"Others find it hard to select a starting point or can't decide a theme to settle on." "You write to communicate to the hearts and minds of others what's burning inside you." (This is getting closer!)

My personal circumstances changed recently because of age and some health issues which meant a limitation on my physical mobility. To add to this was the onset of the coronavirus pandemic which meant a cutting down of my usual activities. It was then I thought this is my chance to write that book.

I was very much attracted by the idea of writing about *ordinary life*. About the elements that form part of our daily existence: work, family and social life, etc.

They are topics we often hear about from different sources and in different contexts. There is a lot behind the environment of a work situation, family histories, traditions and relationships. I thought that along with my own considerations, experiences, anecdotes and relevant quotations about the theme, I would include other stories, some of them written by the protagonists themselves, about their outlook on life, their experiences, their hopes, etc. *"The modern man listens more willingly to witnesses than to teachers."* St. Paul VI, *Evangelii nuntiandi n. 41.*

Getting inside the lives of ordinary people can help us discover the treasures and the wealth of wisdom behind them, often hidden from others, and perhaps in some cases stimulating a change of attitude.

In recent years I have read two books which made an impact on me and that I recall now as relevant in relation to my topic. Both authors in their approaches to life could be considered as an embodiment of people who understand the importance of ordinary life. One of the books, entitled *Small is Beautiful* with the subtitle *A study of economics as if people mattered.* The book is a collection of essays by Fritz Schumacher, a German-born British economist. It was ranked among the hundred most influential books since World War II by the *Times Literary Supplement* in 1995.

According to Barbara Wood, Schumacher's daughter, *"…he spoke to the deep longings inside ordinary people: to their longing for fulfilling creative work, to their search for meaning, to their desire for peace, beauty and permanence. …. He spoke in the context of everyday human life and activity: the workplace, the marketplace, and the living environment.* (Foreword, *Small is Still Beautiful,* Joseph Pearce)

In his book, Schumacher recognises some flaws in economic thinking. The following is an example*: "Above anything else there is a need for a proper philosophy of work which* *understands work not as that which it has become, an inhuman chore as soon as possible to be abolished by automation, but as something decreed by Providence for the good of man's body and soul. Next to the family, it is work and the relationships established by work that are the true foundations of society." (Small is Beautiful,* Ch. 1, p.32)

The second book was written by Joseph Pearce, the English-born American who has authored many books, including biographies. Pearce re-visits Schumacher's arguments with his book entitled *Small is Still Beautiful*. This is subtitled *As if families mattered*. It examines the ways in which they matter today more than ever. Pearce examines the relevance of how small is still beautiful in the 21st century. He discusses the call for a scaling down of the Western pursuit of wealth, and the need to change values in order to protect the earth and the human soul. He is currently involved in what he calls "A journey on the adventure of evangelizing the culture through the power of goodness, truth and beauty" on the internet. He entitled this project: *Nurturing and nourishing a new Catholic revival in the Arts.*

The titles and subtitles of their books prompted me to divide my own book into the three areas mentioned above, which are good settings for a Christian life to develop: The Workplace, The Family and Friendships. Also, the concept of *Small is Beautiful* is an attractive one which can be applied to so many situations in life as we will see through the stories related ahead.

Barbara Wood wrote a biography of her father, while Pearce wrote his own biography. Their approaches – and some incidents in their own lives – are useful to illustrate

INTRODUCTION

some points that I will make. Economic theories and approaches come and go but the ideas that prompted these two to write are perennial. An interesting fact here is how both people experienced an astounding conversion to the Catholic faith after many years of searching for the truth.

In Wood's book, she speaks about her father's decision to become a Catholic:

"In the spring of 1971 he asked Vreni [his wife] to go to Father Scarborough and tell him he wanted to be received into the Catholic Church. It was strange that a man who was used to conversing with presidents should find it necessary to use an intermediary in order to arrange a talk with the local parish priest. And it was probably even stranger to Fritz to be told that Father Scarborough had taken a dim view of his indirect approach and had merely retorted, 'He'd better come himself if he is interested.' For some months after this Fritz went every Wednesday morning to receive instruction from Father Scarborough.

He did not complain that he already knew the content of his talks after years of study and reading. On September 29th 1971 Fritz was received into the Catholic Church. He was very moved as he recited the Creed and received Holy Communion. He had at last come to rest after a long and restless search. He had, as he put it, 'made legal a long-standing illicit love affair.'"

In his biography, Joseph Pearce talks about his own experience:

"In so far as my reception into the Catholic Church was a homecoming, it was also a consummation. It was the culmination of the journey from racial hatred to rational love. It was the end of my life, in the sense that it was the fulfilment of its end, its purpose. And yet at the

4

same time it was also the beginning of a new life in communion with Christ in His Church."

My career, in fact, was music but I never finished my studies, nor did I fulfil my ambition of becoming a concert pianist. When I was in my final year at college in Barcelona, I joined Opus Dei. But this was not the problem. The usual thing for a person who decides to join Opus Dei – or the Work as it is sometimes called – is to continue one's studies and go on to pursue whatever career one wishes. Some members of Opus Dei are needed for government and administrative work, but these are very few and it is usually only for a period of time.

In my case, shortly after I joined I was asked if I would like to go to Ireland and I was very excited with the idea. My plan was to do the B.Mus at University College, Dublin and continue to improve on the piano. Things turned out differently as so often happens in life. We were setting up a residence for university students in Dublin, and it was a question of 'all hands on deck.' In the process, I learned a lot about interior decoration and other interesting things. In my long life in Ireland, I have had the opportunity of being involved with different people, in different circumstances.

"Work is a gift from God and bears witness to the dignity of man, to his dominion over creation. It is an opportunity to develop one's personality. It is a bond of union with others, the way to support one's family, a means of aiding in the improvement of the society in which we live and the progress of all humanity. It is well to remember that the dignity of work is based on Love. Man's privilege is to be able to love and to transcend what is fleeting and ephemeral. This is why man ought not to limit himself to material production."

St. Josemaría Escrivá *(Christ is Passing By)*

CHAPTER 1

THE WORKPLACE

The greater part of time in the life of a mature person is devoted to professional work. There is no stigma nor punishment attached to work. As someone once wrote: 'work is a noble human reality.' As we know, God placed the first man in Paradise so that he would work.

Work, then, is part of life and all it brings with it. We encounter fulfilment, enjoyment, opportunities, etc. and, of course, suffering, disappointments, failures. It is also a way of serving, as in reality all work, no matter what kind, is a service. Much has been written about work and it is good to make use of the many helpful resources to go deeper in understanding all its aspects.

The work of every individual unfolds within a whole series of circumstances, unexpected events, etc., which are also part of life. As a background to work situations, family and friendships, the following considerations might help:

'The normal', 'the ordinary' – words we are very familiar with during the time this book is written. We are going through the Covid 19 pandemic that has assailed the whole world in a way people find hard to believe. *Normal* now is used to convey different meanings – the *new normal*, the *next normal* ... I would not dare to define what the word means as it has different meanings for different people at different times. We can certainly say that at this present moment, life is anything *but* normal.

There are some facts, however – call them natural, or some other more suitable name – that have always been there even though some people may not know them, may not believe them or choose to ignore them. These facts don't change.

The following are a few that come to mind:

- The fact that we are created by God: *"Every spiritual soul is created immediately by God and is immortal."* (Catechism of the Catholic Church n. 366)

- The fact that we were created free: *"God created man a rational being, conferring on him the dignity of a person who can initiate and control his own actions."* (Catechism of the Catholic Church n. 1730)

- We were all born into a family: *"A man and a woman united in marriage, together with their children, form a family."* (CCC n.

CHAPTER 1: THE WORKPLACE

2202). From this, many consequences follow – children and their needs, the needs of society, the wellbeing of the married couple, etc.

- Another issue common to all is the fact that we are born in a country, a specific region with its special characteristics, and a culture, all of which constitute our nationality.

- Love for the country where we were born is a positive thing and should be fostered. Promoting culture and traditions is a way to find a common language. Speaking on the topic of culture, Pope Francis in his *Apostolic Exhortation Evangelii Gaudium* 115, writes: *"Culture embraces the totality of a people's life. Each people in the course of its history develops its culture with legitimate autonomy. This is due to the fact that the human person, by nature, stands completely in need of life in society, finding there a concrete way of relating to reality."*

- Finally, the fact that we have a natural tendency towards, or desire for truth. *"It is in accordance with their dignity that all men, because they are persons... are both impelled by their nature and bound by a moral obligation to seek the truth."* (CCC n. 2467)

We find that without realising or acknowledging it, people tend to act or think according to the above principles. As St. Paul wrote: *"When Gentiles who have not the law do by nature what the law requires, they are the law to themselves, even though they do not have the law. They show that what the law requires is written on their hearts, while their conscience also bears witness, and their conflicting thoughts accuse or perhaps excuse them."* (*Romans* 2:14, 15)

During the pandemic, we have experienced how people have had recourse to means whereby they could diminish its negative impact. People have made use of things like poetry, music, art to help them relax, think more positively, and help others to do as well.

The following lines from a poem written by Fr. Richard Hendrick, OFM (Ordo Fratrum Minorum), which was published in the *Sunday Independent* on 14 March 2020, is a good example of how art and literature can confer serenity and peace on the soul.

Lockdown

Yes, there is fear
Yes, there is isolation
Yes, there is panic
Yes, there is sickness
Yes, there is death
But,
(........)
They say that in the streets of Assisi
People are singing to each other
Across the empty squares
Keeping their windows open
So that those who are alone
May hear the sounds of family around them
(........)
All over the world people are slowing down and reflecting
All over the world people are looking at their neighbours in a new way
All over the world people are waking up to a new reality
To how big we really are
To how little control we really have

To what really matters
To Love
So, we pray, and we remember that
Yes, there is fear
But there does not have to be hate
Yes, there is isolation
But there does not have to be loneliness
Yes, there is panic buying
But there does not have to be meanness
Yes, there is sickness
But there does not have to be disease of the soul
Yes, there is even death
But there can always be a rebirth of love
Wake to the choices you make as to how to live now.
(……..)
Open the windows of your soul
And though you may not be able to touch across the empty square,
Sing

Social media recorded that soon after this poem appeared in the *Irish Independent* it had been shared more than half million times on Twitter, translated into fifteen languages and read aloud on BBC and CNN news programmes. The following day after the poem had been published, Brother Richard commented that when he looked at his phone, he found that it had exploded with messages about the fact that the poem had gone all over the world. He even got a message from a friar in America advising him that 'this is a poem you might like'!

But as we well know, not everything is straightforward or simple in this life. Together with the difficulties, disappointments, we also find the tsunamis, the earthquakes, the pandemics that exist. Either way, we can find comfort in the fact that God loves each one of us, even those who do not love him or know him. And this applies to everyone: we are children of God, and He never abandons us, even when we abandon him. But we need to ask him for things as He always respects our freedom. So, when we experience suffering, we can make use of the resources available: prayer, abandonment, trust. Perhaps a good conversation with a friend might help sort things out.

On the theme of suffering, and indeed unexpected death, I was also impressed by the reaction of the 150 people who were faced with what they thought was imminent death when, in 2009, a short two-hour flight from New York to Charlotte landed in the Hudson River.

A reporter entitled this event *The Miracle of the Hudson.*

Even though most of the passengers were not aware of the full nature of the problem, the inevitable fact for most of them was that they were going to die. Many of the passengers had witnessed birds getting trapped in both engines and they knew the consequences of the situation.

William Prochnau and Laura Parker wrote a book entitled: *Miracle on the Hudson – The Extraordinary Real Life Story Behind Flight 1549, by the Survivors.* In the book, they gather comments from the passengers and describe the atmosphere on the plane during the last minutes of the ordeal.

One thing most of them did was pray. Everyone – Catholics, Christians, Muslims, Jews. One could hear the *Our Father* repeated again and again. Here are random comments from some of the passengers related in their book:

CHAPTER 1: THE WORKPLACE

Ramsey: "Please, God, don't take me today."

Lockhart: "I wasn't, like, frantic, I kept telling myself: 'I'm going to die, wow, I'm going to die, (......) I'm going to die! It was like an event, but I was very much at peace with dying."

Jeff Kolodjay, team leader of a group of golfers also on the plane: "Selfishly I said to myself 'make this painless!'"

Lightner, a highly driven professional woman in the fashion world: "Forgive me for everything I have done wrong. I haven't time to go through it all because I am going to die."

King and Gray were going to get married soon and were holding hands.

King: "Please God help us through this."

Gray: "Lord, please deliver us, and get us through this mess somehow."

Denise Lockie looked up from her brace position: "Are we in Heaven?"

Mark Hood responded: "No, I'm no angel. Come on, we've got to go!"

Someone said: "They tell me your life is supposed to flash in front of your eyes."

And so on ....

In the Manhattan Terminal, Mark Hood dropped to one knee and said a quick prayer. He was so overcome he could barely speak. "I can't believe this has just happened."

Which led to another round of questions: Why did it happen? Why were we all spared?

Tripp Harris, another passenger, went to see his pastor in the hope of finding an answer: "If God wanted us to live, then why didn't he just move the birds out of the way?" The pastor said: "This was a time when everyone around the world needed a miracle."

Why suffering?
What happens after death?
What is the purpose of our life?
Is there an afterlife?
Why does God allow suffering?
Why is there evil in the world?

These and similar questions are often asked, and we don't have full answers, as they are partly a mystery we cannot fully grasp.

Bishop Barron of the Diocese of Winona-Rochester (MN) and founder of Word on Fire, has often been asked these questions.

He explains that God in his providence permits evil, disaster, etc. to bring a greater good. The cruelty of a Stalin or a Hitler, he says, is a product of the freedom God has given us, and also an abuse of that freedom.

He tells of an experience he had when he was parish priest. A young dad came to see him, distraught about an incident he had had with his three-year-old son. He had to bring him to the hospital for major surgery. After the operation, he was trying to explain to his son why he had to go through all that suffering but his son couldn't understand him and kept looking at him in a bewildered manner. Bishop Barron used it as an analogy of God's relationship with us and pointed out the fact that there is a difference.

In the first chapter of the Book of Genesis in the Bible, we find an explanation for the reason suffering and death

CHAPTER 1: THE WORKPLACE

came into the world. We are reminded of this throughout the year when we participate in the liturgy.

It is a good and 'healthy' exercise to remind ourselves from time to time about what is called The Last Things. Pope Benedict XVI in his Encyclical *Pro Spes Salvi* (n. 12) says: *"Eternal life should not be seen as a continuous succession of days of the calendar, but as a moment to submerge ourselves in oceans of limitless love, in which time — before and after — no longer exists."*

But all these situations mentioned above are extraordinary events and are not the normal. However, by looking at them we can learn many lessons. The 'normal' for most of us, most of the time, will be our ordinary life as it unfolds every day: the work we have to do with its ups and downs, our relationships with other people, the difficulties on a small scale which appear from time to time in any one day.

It is good to remember that God wants our happiness here on earth, also. He died so that we might live, He suffered, so that we might be happy. This serenity and joy shows in the personality of people who try to practice the virtue of cheerfulness, spreading peace and joy around them.

To remind ourselves of this aspect of our lives, the founder of Opus Dei wanted a cross without a crucified Jesus to be installed in the oratories of the centres where the numerary members of Opus Dei live.

He explains the meaning in point 178 of his book, *The Way*:

"When you see a poor wooden cross, alone, uncared for and of no value ... and without its crucified, don't forget that that cross is your cross: the cross of each day, that hidden cross without splendour or consolation ... the cross which is awaiting the crucified it lacks: and that crucified must be you."

On the feast-day when the Church celebrates the

Exaltation of the Holy Cross, this cross of wood is decorated with flowers, another reminder that joy is very much part of our life, and that it is possible, even amidst the difficulties we were talking about before, to maintain our peace and joy.

We have heard a lot during the Covid 19 pandemic about being positive and optimistic, and we have witnessed many cases in which people have displayed sterling examples of courage – and indeed ingenuity – to try and maintain a sense of optimism among those around them. It doesn't mean fooling ourselves with negative realities, but living with the decision – which in a Christian is inspired by trust in God – that it is worthwhile making the effort to live in a cheerful way.

Perhaps words from Jesus might help us: *"Do not be anxious about tomorrow for tomorrow will be anxious for itself. Let the day's own trouble be sufficient for the day."* (Mt 6:34, RSVCE)

The Value of Rest

There is an Italian saying which goes as follows: 'Quando il corpo sta bene, l'anima balla.' (When the body is well, the soul dances.) This proverb has innate wisdom. Every person needs to rest, they need to recover the physical strength that is used in their work.

The modern frenzy of 'multi-tasking' may be useful if approached wisely. For example, if we can keep in mind the idea that rest can be a useful job to be performed, or a change of occupation.

Sometimes rest can be a way to take into account other people's needs. It can be an opportunity to organise an outing, a holiday, or take off for a few days when overworked. Take up hobbies, reading, listening to music, sports or any of the many other activities which are available. I came across some suggestions for music lovers about combining some of these tasks: listening to classical music while relaxing, studying or reading. Composers such as Mozart, Debussy, Corelli, Chopin were mentioned as suitable.

It can be very rewarding to make good use of this 'useless time' as Bishop Barron calls it. In a conversation which appears on his website, he suggests that we should distinguish between leisure activities and trivial or frivolous activities. He maintains that the things that matter in life could seem 'useless,' such as parents looking after their kids, playing with them; going for a meal with a friend, spending some time in conversation; sitting on a bus, travelling by plane, etc. Why take out the mobile, the computer? Can we not give a bit of time to just thinking, taking note of our surroundings, talk to the person beside us?

But let us now go to the stories which illustrate some of the points made about work and ordinary life.

They are stories of ordinary people, living an ordinary life. Example is the best teacher as I have mentioned before.

Niamh Walsh

Niamh Walsh is an Irish woman who now lives in Oxford. She writes about her experiences of working and living in the world of international affairs:

"I have spent the past fifteen years working in the field of human rights and international affairs, and I am now a coach and mentor in this area.

When I started working with my internships, I was so

excited that I could make a difference in the world and bring about change for the better. I wanted to put all the years of study and all that I had learned into practice. I was idealistic but had little experience of how complex world geo-politics are, and the limitations of any one organisational response.

Through the years, I have experienced the highs and lows of a professional career. I have often worked long hours in difficult circumstances and have lived in different countries in order to take on new roles. There have been so many challenges and disappointments along with the thrill of being involved in things that truly matter, such as implementing peace agreements between different countries.

Along the way, my Christian faith has been like a 'home away from home', the one certainty in an ever-changing professional landscape. Wherever I have lived abroad, being able to walk into a church and reflect a while has provided a grounding factor in an otherwise uncertain environment.

As I moved jobs and moved countries, I needed to be able to make friends quickly, and adapt to a new culture. All that I had learned from my faith about the importance of friendship, and how to be a good friend, became key to my overall happiness.

In a world where building and leveraging your network is crucial to moving up in your career, I was grateful for all that I had been taught about genuine friendship, including truly giving yourself to others, and striving for what's best for them. This enabled me to create a 'second' family of close friends in each new place I lived. This made the celebration of all the major holidays much more rewarding, and I now am blessed to have good friends scattered across the globe.

Understanding the true nature of friendship also meant that I made huge efforts to maintain my close friendships at home. This was a challenge for me, as family and professional commitments meant people had less available time, but it was so worth every effort I made. You maintain a sense of self-identity when you have friends in your circle that have known and loved you for a very long time, some over thirty years!

Overall, the biggest impact of my Christian faith on my professional career has been the fact of growing to understand how work can be a service to God and to others. Given my particular field of work, I have not had problems seeing the greater meaning of my work, but sometimes on a day-to-day level, one can feel that what we are doing doesn't make that much difference, and that the challenges we face are too great to make any genuine impact on our world.

The vision we take on our work can be altered when we come to realise that by playing our part and doing our bit, real change can and will occur.

Now, while I coach people who want to improve and get more from their lives, I can see first-hand the positive effects that one person can make. My work now is on a smaller scale, but no less fruitful.

Elisabetta, a librarian in Milan

Elisabetta, who runs a large library in Milan, told her story in a local magazine. She is a Catholic, with a strong commitment to living her Christian life to the full. She is married with two children. When her first child arrived, she decided to continue with her professional work but she reduced the number of hours. The second child brought new challenges to her day:

"Being able to dedicate time to planning my day, for example, meals, the shopping list, cleaning, exercise, seeing a friend, requires putting order in the day.

Like many other families with children, the end of the day is one of the most challenging times, especially when both parents are working. The evening brings more tasks with it such as organising the children – baths, supper, singing for my youngest child until he falls asleep."

Directing a large library requires interacting with many colleagues and borrowers every day. When tensions arise, Elisabetta says: "I try not to get upset at people and to be as calm as possible, imitating the example of Our Lord, who was always so patient when the Apostles asked questions which showed their lack of understanding of his teachings. If I find it hard to do so, I try to avoid confronting the person right away, and seek out a solution to the problem before addressing the one responsible for it. I also try to keep smiling!"

Elisabetta realises that it is important to ask help from Our Lord given that she must care for her family and work in the library, just like many other mothers who work outside the home. She has even programmed her smartphone to remind her to say a brief aspiration or prayer throughout the day. This also helps her feel at peace.

CHAPTER 1: THE WORKPLACE

Maria Requena, a nurse from Cartagena who specialised in palliative care

Maria Requena worked in the Hospital of Santa Lucia in Cartagena, Spain. She studied in the University of Murcia and did a Masters in the University of Navarre in Pamplona. There, she studied the works of Cicely Saunders, a British doctor and philosopher who founded the modern hospice movement. Dame Cicely Saunders was responsible for establishing the discipline and culture of palliative care. She introduced effective pain management, and insisted that dying people needed dignity, compassion and respect as well as scientific methodology in the testing of treatments.

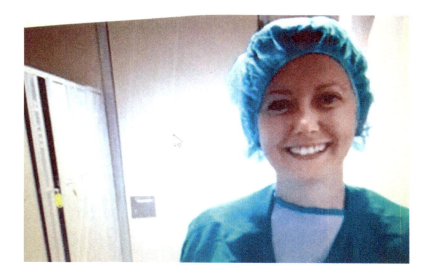

Maria spent many years looking after cancer patients. On one occasion, she said that "when a person who suffers a serious illness asks to be terminated, it is because everything else has failed. It is a failure, not of the person but of the system, which has not been able to look after them as they deserved."

Besides her specialised work as a palliative nurse, she taught in the nursing school and became a volunteer of Medical Assistant Services. After her death in July 2020, she received the 2020 prize of 'Persona Voluntaria' (Voluntary Persons).

In 2016, Maria was involved in the project 'Secunda Smile' (the Second Smile Project), an NGO that promotes "raising awareness of thyroid cancer through random acts of kindness". At a national level, the project was innovative and pioneering in the whole area of palliative care. It also included the training of volunteers about caring for the patients.

When she became sick with cancer herself, Maria opened a help line to clarify the debate on euthanasia, which was a current topic in Spain. With her professional expertise, she put a lot of effort into this, trying to encourage those who might have lost the desire to live. This was her contribution to the imminent project of legalising euthanasia in Spain, which, as we write, has been legalised.

Her blog has been a source of peace for all those people who suffer. Through it, many have shared their fears, physical sufferings, worries and experiences, so that "between us all, we may learn how to be happy in the moment of pain."

Driving for a Change

This is the title of an article which appeared on the Opus Dei website. It is about the Luan University Centre in the Philippines. The volunteers in the centre undertook the job of distributing food and care packages to the drivers of small buses – called jeepneys – and their families, whose income was drastically cut by the pandemic restrictions.

Due to the quarantine restrictions, many people opted to stay at home, and therefore jeepney drivers were left without passengers who were their daily source of income.

Before the pandemic, a jeepney driver would get about 2000 Philippine pesos daily, which is roughly 40 US dollars. Now on a good day they would take 200 pesos. It was a challenge for drivers to provide basic needs and education for their families. The transition to online classes during the pandemic required devices and digital connections that were beyond their means.

Consequently, the students of Luan organised an Outreach programme with the objective of providing care packages to 70 families. The response of companies and friends to the Outreach drive was very generous and encouraging.

One email which was sent to the Philippine Food Bank Foundation got a positive response in less than 20 minutes. A businessman, who himself experienced the negative impact of the quarantine, sent a donation. "We are all in the same boat," he said. "Thank you for the opportunity to help."

Donations in kind such as rice, cooking oil, margarine, soya and cookies also arrived. Another generous donor promptly supplied funds for the mobile phone load, which the children of the drivers needed for their online classes.

Student volunteers prepared 85 sacks with 10kg of rice and 85 eco bags with assorted food items.

A week later, following the usual health protocol, the students helped to host a simple programme with light-hearted games and prizes. It all ended with smiles and laughter that cheered everyone up.

The volunteers were especially grateful for the experience, as they believed they had benefited as much as the drivers and their families. One simple outcome was the realisation that we were never born to live for ourselves alone, but for others, and with others.

The volunteers of Luan University Centre on the way to distributing the sacks

The volunteers of Luan University Centre acknowledging their donors

CHAPTER 1: THE WORKPLACE

Story of a Portuguese Horseman (taken from the Opus Dei website)

A Portuguese Horseman with his wife

Miguel's passion has always been for horses. His family owns a discotheque. He tells his own story:

"My name is Miguel. I live in Lisbon and am 40 years old. I was born into a very normal family with two other siblings. Up to 12th grade, I attended the Abrantes Rural Development School and specialised in horse management. Upon graduating, I went to France to study with a professional rider. I did everything from the most basic grooming tasks to riding beautiful show horses. Horse riding has always been my passion.

I returned from France both naïve and arrogant, as I thought I was already a great horseman. I became a bit wild. I went out almost every night with friends from the world of horses. I had several girlfriends but was determined not to commit myself to anyone.

I gave up practising my religion and stopped going to Mass. At 22 years, I had lost my faith, but I was still seeking God without realising it. I started having sessions with an astrologer who had a reputation for helping many people. Among the many suggestions he gave me, one was quite surprising: to go to Mass for eight days in a row.

However, I continued with my wildlife, but I still had a great desire to be an excellent horseman.

One day, back in 2011, a cousin invited me to lunch with a priest called Fr. Hugo. I had a conversation with this priest which had a huge impact on me. So much so, that immediately I asked him to hear my confession. I unburdened myself of a ton of weight in that confession and realised that until then I had been living in darkness.

After that, I met a woman called Maria, and I soon sensed that she was the person I wanted to spend the rest of my life with. We now have three beautiful children.

A friend of mine told me about Opus Dei's activities of Christian formation. I soon realised that I had found my vocation in life. The activities offered me all the spiritual help that I needed and also showed me the way to live as a child of God. I also learned how to draw closer to God in my daily life, in my family, my work, and dedicating myself to other people.

In 2019, I was diagnosed with multiple myeloma (a malignant tumour of the bone marrow). What I thought was simply a shoulder injury from my profession as a horse rider was actually blood cancer, a disease for which there is still no cure.

My first thought was that if Jesus gave his life and died for me, why shouldn't I suffer for him? God granted me the grace not to become angry or fall into despair. From that moment on, my life took on a new value. The illness and

CHAPTER 1: THE WORKPLACE

suffering served to draw me closer to Jesus than ever before.

In 2020, I was admitted to the Portuguese Cancer Institute in Lisbon in the middle of the Covid pandemic. I couldn't receive any visitors, but I was lucky to receive Communion from the hospital chaplain every day.

I went through some very difficult days as I experienced a lot of pain and had complicated treatments. In the middle of everything, I had the support of Maria and my family, as well as my friends and my brothers in the Work (Opus Dei), and many people who were praying for me.

The fact that I have confronted such difficult challenges in my life and can still be deeply happy has no explanation. I ask myself: what can it be, but God's grace?"

Gabrielle Doyle, librarian in Dublin

"Let me introduce myself: I am a retired librarian and like many retirees, I am busier than ever! When I retired, I continued my involvement in the formative activities organised by the Opus Dei Prelature and I became a volunteer with Brosna Educational Centres, (a charity operating initiatives across Ireland for the advancement of education, and which gives a particular focus to foster solidarity and awareness of the needs of others in the service of society).

I also studied the History of European Painting at UCD. On completion of the course, I applied to be a volunteer with the Visitors Experience Team at the National Gallery of Ireland and was accepted. This volunteering role is to support staff in delivering a high level of visitor-focused experience at the information desks and in the gallery. Each volunteer works for a few hours every week at the information desk. It is in the context of volunteering with the National Gallery that I wish to contribute to the idea that small is beautiful.

Gabrielle Doyle (on the right) explaining the gallery floor plan to a visitor to the National Gallery, Dublin

The National Gallery belongs to the people of Ireland, and everyone is welcome, including small visitors. The Educational Department's vision is to inspire, encourage and support learning through art. It is a joy to see groups of small primary school children sitting on the floor in front of a painting while a NGI tour guide interacts with them about the painting in front of them. Who knows what small seeds of creativity are being nurtured as they gaze around them?

George Bernard Shaw acknowledged the formative effect the Gallery had on him. When he made the National Gallery

CHAPTER 1: THE WORKPLACE

a beneficiary of his will, he said that he owed to it much of the only real education he ever got as a boy in Dublin.

The National Gallery is one of the country's most popular free visitor attractions. It is a delightful sight to see the reaction of visitors who approach the information desk with their purse or card in their hand and being told that entrance to the permanent collection and some exhibitions is free. What an encouragement for the public to return and enjoy their Gallery!

The National Gallery has a strong accessibility policy for visitors with disabilities and for those with reduced mobility. The availability of wheelchairs for use in the Gallery, the noise cancelling headphones for children with autism and many other facilities all contribute to an enjoyable visit. We, the volunteers, need to know what is available to them and their carers, even the canine ones. I have to admit that I was volunteering for some time before I realised that the aluminium bowls that were under the information desks were for water for the guide/carer dogs!

There are usually two volunteers at the information desks, and we are the welcoming faces for the visitors, maintaining our culture of the *"Céad Mile Fáilte"* (*A Hundred Thousand Welcomes*) to everyone who comes through the entrance. I particularly like it when people who live in Dublin come and admit that this is their first visit – they have never been here before. We hope it won't be their last visit.

It always helps me to think of the uniqueness of each person, patiently listening to their questions, without interrupting or finishing off their question for them. A small point but it is important to listen carefully. There are always new and unusual questions. An American leaving the Gallery came up to the desk rather excited and asked whether it was true that our painting by Claude Monet was actually the picture painted by Monet. I was puzzled – I hadn't heard this question before. I said yes, it was the one painted by Monet and that the paintings in the Gallery were painted by the artists themselves. He got very excited and said he was going back to look at it again. He explained that the Gallery in his hometown, had only prints/copies of the originals!

St. Josemaría, in *The Way*, says, "Don't make negative criticism: if you can't praise say nothing." (*The Way*, no. 443). This is a healthy maxim to follow in all working environments. If something needs to be improved, there are usually proper channels in place and procedures that can be followed. Positivity helps our colleagues and our visitors. Sure, many things can be improved; we don't like certain things, ways of doing things, but there are always positive points, and we can turn situations around and look for the silver lining in them, even if it is a small point.

There is a saying that a smile is the best make-up you can wear, and I've noticed that a smile to visitors as they leave the Gallery very often is reciprocated with another smile and they end their visit on a positive note.

Unfortunately, due to the Covid pandemic, the volunteer role has stopped temporarily since March 2020. Now there are people working at contact tracing at the information desk. We are eagerly waiting the news of the date when the volunteers can return.

CHAPTER 1: THE WORKPLACE

After the canonisation of Saint Josemaría Escrivá (founder of Opus Dei,) Saint John Paul II said in the homily at the Mass of Thanksgiving:

"St. Josemaría was chosen by the Lord to announce the universal call to holiness, and to point out that daily life and ordinary activities are a path to holiness."

Considering the importance of work for every individual and for society, it is not surprising that in the 20th century God wanted Opus Dei (the international organisation) to appear in the world (1928), with the mission to spread the Christian message that every person is called to holiness and that every honest work can be sanctified. In the book "Conversations with Josemaría Escrivá", he says: *"Those who are called, wish to dedicate themselves freely and responsibly to look for holiness and carry out their apostolate in the middle of the world, committing themselves to live a specific spirit and to receive throughout their lives a special kind of formation."*

"The recognition of the family as the unity of the State is the kernel of Distribution. The insistence on ownership to protect its liberty is the shell. We that are Christians believe that the family has a divine sanction. But any reasonable pagan, if he will work it out, will discover that the family existed before the State and has prior rights; that the State exists only as a collection of families, and that its sole function is to safeguard the rights of each and all of them."

G.K. Chesterton.

CHAPTER 2

THE FAMILY

I had been thinking of starting this chapter with a definition of the family I found a few years ago, written in one of the documents of the European Courts of Human Rights. I just could not find it among my notes, diaries, or anywhere among my papers. I resorted to Google and could not find it there either. I tried definitions in other global organisations with no luck. I realised then that more than likely the former definition had been deleted, and instead some vague, dubious and ambiguous explanations of what constitutes a family are given.

The following are two examples:

From the European Court of Human Rights:
"Men and women of marriageable age have a right to marry, and to found a family according to the national laws governing the exercising of this right. The wording of the Article has been modernised to cover cases in which national legislation recognises arrangements other than marriages to found a family."

United Nations – universal declaration of human rights:
Men and women of full age, without any limitation due to race, nationality or religion, have the right to marry and found

a family. They are entitled to equal rights as to marriage and its dissolution. (…) The family is the natural and fundamental group unit of society and is entitled to protection by society and the State."

There seems to have been a lot comments sent to the United Nations Human Rights office in favour of supporting the longstanding understanding of the family in international law and policy. Other organisations have filed comments that sought to undermine the current situation, so that the meaning of family would include same-sex relationships.

I asked a friend of mine if she might know where I could find a suitable description of the family – if not a definition – among the global organisations. Her husband sent me the link which provided me with the explanation about this, or rather with the reasons why I could not find an explanation.

It came through a conference given in the Population Research Institute in New York City in 1994 by Allan C. Carlson, Ph.D., President of the Rockford Institute, Illinois. The title he gave the conference was "WHAT'S WRONG WITH THE UNITED NATIONS DEFINITION OF THE FAMILY".

Many of the flaws outlined in this conference are still current because of the various kinds of unions that call themselves 'family'.

The opening lines of the conference went like this:

"To control the definition of a thing is to control the thing itself. This was the great insight of Humpty Dumpty in Lewis Carroll's fantasy, Alice in Wonderland. Recall the dialogue: after he defines 'glory' as a nice knock-down argument, Humpty Dumpty explains the point to a doubting Alice: 'When I use a word, it means just what I chose it to mean – neither more nor less.' When Alice responds that the real issue

is whether you can change the meaning of a word to make it mean what you want it to mean, Humpty Dumpty demurs: 'The question is, which one is the master — that's all.'"

Allan Carlson says that *"it is simply false to argue that there is no relatively fixed definition of family. The human record, honestly confronted, shows that the family is a natural, universal, and irreplaceable community, rooted in human nature. The family in all ages and in all corners of the globe can be defined as a man and woman bonded together through a socially-approved covenant of marriage, in order to regulate sexuality, to bear, raise, and protect children, to provide mutual care and protection, to create a small home economy, and to maintain continuity between generations, those going before and those coming after."*

Marriage is not an invention of Christianity or indeed of any religious tradition. In the words of Bishop Kevin Doran, published by *Position Papers* in April 2015: *"Primitive societies recognised the uniqueness of the male-female relationship, written in human nature. Religious faith helps men and women to make a connection between their marital relationship with God, but it does not fundamentally change the meaning and purpose of marriage which was already well established in most cultures long before the arrival of the mainstream religious traditions. They were common almost to every culture. It was faithful; it was associated with the birth and upbringing of children, and it was between a man and a woman."*

The above can help to understand better the true nature of marriage and the commitments attached to it. These commitments demand of each partner a determination not to dialogue about breaking the bond.

In the question of marriage and procreation, Fritz Schumacher has something to tell us. It came through Barbara Wood, his daughter in her book *Alias Papa:*

"Harry, a friend of Fritz, said to him: 'I've got a copy of the latest encyclical of the Pope if you'd like it, Fritz.'

'Is it *Humanae Vitae*?' Fritz asked.

'Yes, it is.'

'I've not only got a copy, but I've read it,' Fritz replied.

'What do you think of it?' asked Harry.

The answer was surprising: 'If the Pope had written anything else, I would have lost all faith in the papacy,' Fritz said."

It is interesting to note that when this episode took place, Schumacher had not yet been received into the Catholic Church.

In the recent encyclical, *Fratelli Tutti,* on Fraternity and Social Friendship published on 3rd October 2020, Pope Francis wrote: *"In a family, parents, grandparents and children all feel at home; no one is excluded. If someone has a problem, even a serious one, even if he brought it upon himself, the rest of the family comes to his assistance; they support him. His problems are theirs. In families, everyone contributes to the common purpose; everyone works for the common good, not denying each person's individuality but encouraging and supporting it. They may quarrel, but there is something that does not change: the family bond. Family disputes are always resolved afterwards. The joys and sorrows of each of its members are felt by all. That is what it means to be a family!"* (*Fratelli Tutti* n. 230).

With his usual, practical ways, Pope Francis provides us with examples and goals for our daily lives.

People usually come into the world within a family. The family has a great responsibility; it has a mission to fulfil, which will have an impact on society, and indeed on the world. It is in the home that we learn how to practise human virtues such as docility, obedience, loyalty, understanding, respect, study, working well, and many others. We also learn to have affection for our parents and siblings.

Bonds can also be created by the environment, our material surroundings – decorations, family photos, preparing meals, family celebrations, etc.

Juan Luis Lorda, a priest of Opus Dei and author of some spiritual books, says in his latest work *Beyond Good Intentions*, p. 91: *"For a human being, these early bonds to persons and things are like the roots of a tree: they feed him, making him grow, situate him in the world. (…) Bonding to a family grafts one into the history of a human group and into a cultural tradition with origins."* It helps to understand the far-reaching effects a good family background can have on their environment.

But there has been much written about the family; I could give a long list of bibliography which would supply ways and means to improve and go deeper in the understanding of the responsibility which God has placed on our parents' shoulders. There have been many World Meetings of Families, which have covered all aspects of family life. Their insights and experiences can be found on the website.

Many popes have written encyclicals and letters which provide the knowledge needed to help Christian families flourish and grow. St. John Paul II wrote the Encyclical *Familiaris Consortio* in November 1981. He also wrote a *Letter to Families* in Feb 1994; the importance of the family is mentioned in many of his writings.

Example is the best teacher

Once more we will have a look at the real-life, real experiences of some families who are trying to bring into the world honest and loyal citizens who can take over posts of responsibility and leadership. We will also take a look at ordinary efforts of families – many of them silent and hidden – who through their daily lives contribute to make this world a better place. In the words of St. Josemaría, those people are *"sowers of peace and joy."*

I like to mention one aspect of my own family which I thought would fit in with the narrative of the book.

One of the characteristics of good family relationships is the fact that its members can maintain the links which united them at the beginning, in spite of the natural changes that unfold with the passing of time. In my family, these changes were quite striking and, in some ways, unexpected as a few of us became scattered around the world in a short time.

Nevertheless, the links that united us at the very beginning of our earthly life have never been broken in spite of the physical distances which separated us, or the changes that came in our different ways of thinking.

We were born and brought up in our early years by my parents in a Christian environment. There were six of us, three girls and three boys, in that order. On Sundays, when we all participated in the Liturgy of Mass, we occupied a whole bench in our parish. We had been encouraged as soon as we reached a suitable age to receive the Sacrament of Penance and Reconciliation. And so, every Saturday morning, we went to confession. We used to say the family rosary, even though occasionally we got the giggles. We also said grace before meals.

As siblings, we have a few things in common. We love music, especially classical music. During the holidays we would stay in a small village near Puigcerda, which was close

CHAPTER 2: THE FAMILY

to the French border. Some evenings we would sing traditional songs together outside the house under the moonlight, accompanied by the banjo or the guitar. We enjoyed pop music and the popular songs of the time.

We also loved mountaineering, sometimes spending two or three days with our friends, camping in the mountains, and trying to reach the highest peaks of the Catalan Pyrenees.

We all did reasonably well in the school, but here also we had something in common: none of us liked maths. We were not good at the subject. We often recall, with hilarity when we meet, an incident related to this which happened in our school. It was a co-ed school, and for a while every year the same maths teacher had one of us in his class. One day (this happened in my class), the teacher asked a question which I answered, probably chancing my arm, much to his amazement and which prompted him to say under his breath "even Montserrat knows it."

Later, at the time of our third level education, life for us took very different turns. My two sisters went to Germany to improve their German. One married James Stewart (another James Stewart) who worked in the American Navy and was posted to the American Base in Munich, and the other married Hans Mayr, the director of a school in the Bavarian region. This meant that they both left Spain, one to live in Washington and the other in Augsburg, Germany.

Their lives changed radically. My youngest brother, Alex, established himself in Paris, having married Pierrette whom he met while studying in the Sorbonne. Sadly, both have passed away recently. My other two brothers, Josep and Albert, remained in Barcelona, and are still living there, one married to Jessica, who is Spanish, and the other to Anne, who comes from Holland. Each of their stories, if published, would make interesting reading. I have already explained at the beginning of this book what I did with my life. This scattering of a family was unusual at the time.

With the passing of time away from the family home, and living in different cultures and surroundings, many changes took place in the lives of each one of us, not only in geographical distance, but also in ways of thinking in areas such as religion, philosophy, ideologies, and various other approaches to life.

Even though we lived in different parts of the world, we met when time and work permitted it, mostly in Barcelona and twice in Paris, especially from the 1980s onwards when my parents had already passed from this life. These reunions included, of course, the happy addition to our family of my three sisters-in-law and my brother-in-law from Germany. My sister in America and her husband decided by mutual agreement to separate some years after their marriage, though he still keeps in touch with his wife, children and grandchildren.

So, the world at large became our family home and the usual ways of family relationships changed somehow, but did not disappear. To this date I can truthfully say that nothing has ever been a barrier or a motive of tension among us. In moments of discussion about issues where we think very differently, our interest in each other's views and the respect for their freedom is always taken into account. Perhaps our natural instinct was not to touch topics where we all knew we had different views.

I am including here a poem in Catalan that my brother Josep wrote in 1994, depicting in some way our situation. I include also the English translation.

Bon mati, Bon mati!
Es desvetlla l'albada
Reprenem el vell cami
Del no-res a l'infinit,
Capvesprol, si Déu vol,
trobarem el repòs,
Si volem, si Déu vol
Lluny dels astres, lluny del desti
Sis germans som brostats
D'una sola brancada
I hem omplert terres I mars
De senyals i d'il.lusions.
Qui ens vulgui acompanyar,
Que prengui el seu cami,
El pas viu, el cap alt,
El sarrall ben alleugerit

The English translation:

In the morning, in the morning
The dawn awakens
We take the old road again
From nothingness to infinity
By nightfall, God willing
We will find rest,
If we are willing, God's willing
Far from the stars, far from destiny
Six siblings sprout,
From a single branch

*We have filled lands and seas
With signs and hopes.
Whoever wants to join us,
Should go his own way,
Brisk pace, head held high,
And the bag light*

To get the translation right, I decided to give the job to professionals and a company in Dublin did it for me. My brother, the author of the poem, thought it sounded very well and modern. When the first draft was sent to me, they had translated the word 'illusions' literally. I pointed out to them that illusions in English had a different meaning; what would they think of the alternatives: 'aspirations' or 'dreams' or 'hopes'? Even though I had it as a third option, they chose 'hopes'. And how right they were! It made me think about how important hope is as it responds to the desires for happiness which we have in our hearts.

I came to Ireland in 1954.

CHAPTER 2: THE FAMILY

With my parents walking near O'Connell street, when they came to see me in the 1960s. With us is my cousin Arnau Torrents (Arnold) who is also a member of Opus Dei and was sent to Ireland by St. Josemaría in the 1950s.

With my brothers and sisters strolling along the Park of Luxembourg, Paris in the 1980s. From left: Josep, Myo (M. Asuncion) Albert, Montse, Alex (Alexandre) and myself.

44

The following account comes from Jennifer Kehoe whom I have known for many years.

Jennifer is married for 26 years and mother of six children aged eleven to twenty-five. She is a regular speaker on topics of marriage and family in both Ireland and UK. She is an occasional freelance writer and has been published in *Position Papers* and various Catholic publications.

I was very happy she shared so much of her own experiences, and I thought it was worthwhile publishing them in full, as they add good insights on the whole area of marriage and family life.

Marriage and Family Life – Jennifer Kehoe

While browsing through Facebook recently I came upon a question, posted for fun, on a page about reading. It asked a simple question:

"Where would you be now had you followed your dreams?"

It is the sort of question which sets a person thinking, regardless of who or where they are on life's journey. What would you be now had you followed your dreams? What were my dreams? How did I envision my future when I was my younger self? I did not have to think too long to come up with my answer. I just had to look in the mirror.

When I was a young child growing up, I remember a little booklet which was around our house for a while. The title was *The Joys and Travails of a Large Family*. I picked this booklet up many times to relish the funny and endearing anecdotes written by the dad of a large family, a supernumerary of Opus Dei. Both

CHAPTER 2: THE FAMILY

my parents were also supernumerary members of Opus Dei.

Jennifer Kehoe with her daughter Louise at home in Naas

Jennifer Kehoe with her family

That family lived in a completely different country and culture to mine, but I recognised the same philosophy which was the core of my own experience. I suppose you could summarise it as a cheerful holiness which had its feet firmly on the ground, encapsulated in the form of a married couple surrounded by children, nappies, copybooks, grocery shopping, family trips … all the ordinary things which make up ordinary life. I loved living in such a family, and I loved reading about that other family; I knew that was exactly what I wanted for my own future. That was precisely my dream.

It might seem strange in our culture for a girl to have such a 'simple' dream and to pursue it, but I have never looked at the desire to be a wife and mother in that way. Today's children may aspire to emulate their heroes, YouTube celebrities, sport icons and so on. In that, I was no different. My heroes were my parents. I admired everything about them, and now with the passing of time, and having life's experience under my own belt, I can say I admire them even more. They knew what it was to suffer, to have worries and concerns, to raise children in a culture which with each passing year grows ever more hostile to Christ and Christianity, and yet they were steadfast, cheerfully witnessing to us, and to anyone who knew them, what it was to be a Christian in the middle of the world.

G.K. Chesterton once wrote: "The most extraordinary thing in the world is an ordinary man and an ordinary woman and their ordinary children."

Chesterton died in 1936, shortly after a young priest, Saint Josemaría Escrivá founded Opus Dei. Both Chesterton and St Josemaría Escrivá's insights about the extraordinary nature of ordinary life mirror each other. St Josemaría's teaching

CHAPTER 2: THE FAMILY

later inspired Pope St John Paul II to call him *The Saint of Ordinary Life*. Most of us are pretty ordinary. We live in ordinary places and do ordinary things. Most of us will not be called to the great heroic deeds which hit the headlines, or go down in annals of history, and yet we can live an everyday heroism which may never be noticed. But God notices, in the same way a mother notices. And that is what I hope to explore in this chapter.

Last year, in the short window of the opening of hotels in the summer, my husband and I booked to spend the night of our silver wedding anniversary at the hotel where we had held our wedding reception. Due to the pandemic, the original older part of the hotel was closed but, in a lovely gesture, the manager asked a staff member to accompany us to look around and suggested we stroll down memory lane at our ease.

Twenty-five years previously, my twenty-three-year-old medical student husband of mere hours and I, along with our families, had laid the first foundations of our lives together at that very spot. The scene could not have been more poignant. Where a sunbathed garden reception had been held on the sloping lawn overlooking the picturesque Blessington Lakes that nestle in the Wicklow mountains, there now stood bushes and a modern extension to the hotel. The access to the lake where my husband's classmates had paddled and skimmed stones to the sunset was now fenced off and overgrown. As though to crown the poignancy, in contrast to the idyllic sunshine of our wedding day, a persistent rain fell. We stood in silence, arm in arm, under a shared umbrella, the trees dripping memories, in one of those moments where words would have been an invasion. I remember the wordless thoughts I had during that moment: John has seen what I've seen, and he knows.

This man standing beside me in the rain has seen what I have seen: the torrent of memories going through my head were the same ones going through his; it did not need to be said. Twenty-five years of vignettes passed through our shared thoughts: the joys of little babies, their delightful newborn smell, the hours spent contemplating their perfection in what my father once called a preview of the Beatific Vision, the soul-wrenching ache of miscarriage after miscarriage, quibbles over who was more tired ... "You were asleep, I heard you!", daytrips to pet farms, campfires, lost shoes and homework, endless school parent-teacher meetings, angsty teenagers and their struggles.

As we stood, memories of marriage doldrums caused by the low-grade neglect which all too often is the result of busyness floated by, years when we forgot to date because we were too tired or because babysitters were expensive, or "we'll go next week." I guiltily remembered my immature and undeserved silences and slick remarks, and how they had been forgiven immediately by this good man who had never criticised me in twenty-five years. We thought of those wedding guests who had passed away, both my parents, mutual friends, relatives. And especially ... most especially ... we thought about a sick little child, our little girl, who came to our family and showed us just what love really means. And all through that, the common thread binding it all was our marriage. Like the protective umbrella we now stood under, the sacrament of marriage, the family's armour for the world.

In all of this, what stands out is that in our entire marriage, apart from perhaps our sick child and the necessary surgeries

CHAPTER 2: THE FAMILY

and hospitalisations and all that went with that, which itself has evolved into normal life and is now just part of our family's backdrop, nothing in the twenty-five years was spectacular or extraordinary. Our experiences are typical. We are an ordinary man and his ordinary wife, and their ordinary children … the very thing which Chesterton called extraordinary.

Why is such a thing extraordinary? I am convinced that it is because without the foundation of strong family life, nothing can stand. One generation builds on the previous, who themselves built on their previous generation. In the last fifty years (suspiciously aligning with the almost blanket rejection of Humanae Vitae), we have seen the tragic and multiple consequences of the crumbling of culture's foundation which is family. The state of our culture is indeed dire. However, we must remember that God chose you and me for precisely these times, to be here in a crumbling culture as instruments to help rebuild it.

I love the story of the Leaning Tower of Pisa. I will never forget the gasp of breath the first time I passed under the archway leading to the piazza and set eyes on that gravity defying tilt. It is truly astonishing that it is only the ingenuity of man that is preventing the total collapse of this magnificent tower into a pile of rubble. I feel our culture is just like that, it is leaning perilously toward ruination, but with care and ingenuity the collapse can be prevented and perhaps, in individual cases, completely reversed.

Home, marriage, family have long been the 'heart' words of humanity, the words which reach right to the core. Home, marriage and family are the only pillars strong enough to hold up a culture. You may remember the Disney Pixar movie *Inside*

Out released a few years ago in which the little girl's life was portrayed through the eyes of the emotions inside her head. Everything around her seemed to be collapsing as she moved home, changed schools and was growing up. Amid all this, the last man standing, so to speak, was the family, a stable pillar which did not crumble. Whether this depiction of family based on the marriage of one man, one woman was by accident or design, who knows, but I thought it was a powerful message, and one which receives little acclaim in our culture. In our core, home and family are still 'heart words'.

During this last year's lockdowns, how many have longed for home? How many adult children have longed for their parents? We awakened a loneliness for home which we had all but forgotten. In many instances, we re-discovered family life and the warmth of family members delighting in each other. I met a friend of mine one day while out on my two-kilometre stroll. He told me that all four of his young adult daughters were home with them during lockdown. At first the girls railed against the limitations but before long they had re-discovered board games, jigsaws, baking and family meals which had been long abandoned. What a happy father he was telling me these simple things; his family had rediscovered home. That 'heart' word … home.

I recently came upon a magazine article with a photograph showing a man standing beside an excavated piece of land exposing the roots of prairie grass which is native to the American Plains. For comparison, on the other side of the photo was a similar cut-out showing the growth above and below ground of a commercial crop. While both the prairie grass and the grain crop had similar above-ground growth, the roots of the grain plants were mere inches deep. On the other hand, the native plant had roots which burrowed to a depth greater than the man was tall, at least six feet.

Can you imagine the devastation a tornado or summer storm would do to the ground with the commercial crop? Without the anchoring strength of roots, the soil, along with all the plants would simply wash or be blown away. Nothing, no tornado, no tempest, could usurp the prairie grass; the roots intertwined with multiple strands can endure even the most ruthless of assaults. Such is the strength of family; it is precisely the intertwined deep foundation which protects. Even prairie fires, such as is described so terrifyingly by Laura Ingalls Wilder, merely damage the surface, and what looks like ruination ends up instead providing nourishment for new life and new growth.

Home is not simply a convenient set-up where dinner is served, the rent is free and where clean clothes magically appear in one's wardrobe. Home runs much deeper than that. Home is precisely where children get their identity, where roots feed the shoots. I have an ornamental wooden sign in my house which was a gift from my sister. It reads *Home is Where Memories Are Made and Cherished Forever*; our children's memories are more than fleeting thoughts, they are a big part of what they are. If the root is healthy, so will the shoot be healthy and fruitful.

When I had my first child, I used to buy the occasional parenting magazine for advice and tips. It was not until several babies later that I realised that the journalists writing these magazines knew little or nothing about babies, and much less about family life. However, somewhere along the way I read a piece of advice which clicked with me, and which I have passed on to many new parents since: babies are designed for amateur parents. What a liberating piece of advice! We do not need to be perfect, we do not need to always succeed, but we do need to care and to try.

Most of our children were quite cautious by nature. They generally required lots of parental encouragement and reassurance in order to try new things. The first time we brought them on a holiday outside Ireland, I was anxious that they should try as many new experiences as possible. The campsite we stayed on had a wonderful waterpark designed for families. Our cautious children were reluctant to try out the waterslides even though they looked like a lot of fun. I enthusiastically assured them they would love it, the other children were doing it, I would be there at the bottom ... I would catch them ...

With that guarantee, the four eldest all agreed. Up they went and I positioned myself at the bottom of the slide, ready to save each child from a watery fate. The first child positioned herself ... and launched like a cannonball from a gun. I instantly realized there was no way I could possibly catch her!

Before I could take a breath, there she was, ignominiously plunged underwater to the bottom. I hauled the tearful and betrayed child to the surface, and turned to spot the next child hurtle down the chute at great speed, then the next and the next, each one flying gloriously past my feeble arms straight to the bottom of the pool ...

Never one to be too discouraged for long by my parenting fails, my enthusiasm excelled the following year while on a short holiday to the West of Ireland, my paternal ancestral home.

Picture the scene: it is another idyllic sunny day, and the children are busy exploring the granite rock pools, nets and buckets in hand. They sporadically return to their relaxing parents with containers of seawater and various sea treasures: shrimps, shells, seaweed and such like. And then I decided to join them and up the wow factor of their findings. Finding a promising rock pool, I summoned the children – all five at the time – and, hoisting a large granite rock, to the delight of my children, I unearthed a large crab. I emphasise this was not a tiny almost transparent typical rock pool sized crab: it was a large fully grown crab. In the middle of the ensuing impressive lecture on the habitat, lifestyle and diet of crabs, I suddenly realised to my dismay that the granite boulder I had lifted and which was poised precariously over the crab was slowly slipping from my fingers. There was nothing I could do. To the children's horror, and my even greater horror, the heavy boulder broke free and crashed down onto the crab, shooting pieces of claw, shell and … well … everything else that makes up a crab, out in every direction.

I tell these two anecdotes because in both of those moments I felt I had failed. I had been the cause of two rather unpleasant experiences for my children. I had fallen far short of the goal I had set for myself. Rather than scoring, the very goalposts quite literally had come crashing down. However, all these years later, both stories are repeated often and with great aplomb by my now young adult children. They remember only the flawed enthusiasm of their young mother and nothing of the life-altering trauma I suspected I had imposed on them. As I said, children are designed for amateur parents.

On a more serious note, every family and every marriage have dark moments. Worries about employment, health, infertility, relationships, all the problems known to mankind can present themselves within a marriage.

I recently watched a documentary about the forces of nature, particularly focusing on landslides. I love watching such programmes with our children. I love the gasps of astonishment as we witness the moan of the planet in the process of forming its ever-changing landscape. I love seeing the children's eyes wide open and their jaws drop in awe at the close shaves of the cameramen and film makers who have captured these amazing moments. And most of all, I love that I am watching all this from a vantage point which poses us no danger. One clip in the documentary featured two men outrunning a landslide by reversing their jeep at great speed. The two men who were caught up in this race against nature were interviewed and spoke of the adrenalin and the urgency which kicked them into pulling off this great escape. There was no choice. Act or perish were the only two options open to them. So, they acted, and they succeeded.

Most of us will never be caught up in a landslide, or an earthquake, or a volcano. The likelihood of huge events like this hitting us is pretty slim. But just now and again we may get a little glimpse of the big things. Our family faced a big challenge some years ago in the form of a very loved, yet to be born, daughter facing major health issues. It affected our life in a similar way as you would imagine being caught up in a landslide would feel like. Living through that time was difficult, heady, emotionally and spiritually draining, and everything else you can guess it would be.

Several years later, when a normality of sorts had returned

to our family, I was able to look back and evaluate whether we, or more precisely, I, had changed as a result. I think it is fair to say that anybody would be affected in all sorts of ways, most of them probably for the better, after a life-changing event like that. One thing that still jumps out at me whenever I think about it is this: sometimes the BIG thing is easier than the LITTLE thing.

How can it be easier to carry a baby in your womb, not knowing whether she will live or die? How can it be easier to hand a tiny baby over to a cardiac surgeon and place her life in his hands … and to do that repeatedly? How can it be easier to see her being manually bagged by PICU staff and stand there helpless and wondering whether your own heart is ever going to start beating again? Are you *mad*?

It is not easy.

It is not easy at all, it is very, very, very difficult. I am definitely not saying it is easy. What I am saying, though, is that it was like being caught up in the landslide. It was terrible, but easy to get up and get on with it because there was no choice. That adrenalin which forces the decision … fight or flight … fight or flight … No decision to be made there: fight was the only option.

There was the God-given grace which came our way. There was the love and support which was doled out to us without reserve from near and far. There were emails, text messages, Facebook notes, letters, cards, masses, candles, flowers … and food.

In some ways, however difficult it was, we were along for the ride. We did not really have to do anything. We were carried along by the landslide. The burden was shared.

Now compare that to a dreary day at home when the children are at school. There is nothing in the fridge with which to make dinner and you need to go to the supermarket. Of all the housekeeping chores, the one I hate most is grocery shopping. I hate it! Give me an ironing board and a load of fresh-scented laundry any day.

Compare that to 9pm on a midweek evening. Husband is at a meeting; the children really should be in bed and there is a general air of untidiness around the place. I am enjoying a chat with a faraway friend on Facebook and sitting nice and comfy in my chair by the fire.

Compare that to the mid-afternoon slump. I clearly remember that I promised Jesus I would factor him in today because – I was so sorry – I had left him out yesterday (and the day before), but I'm so tired and sluggish, and I still haven't put on dinner, and there's all these children ... with homework!

Oh dear ... Jesus ... do you mind if I put you on the long finger ... again?

Compare that to mulling over that imagined slight your husband made of you this morning ... mulling over it all day, whereby it has grown out of all proportion, and he had better be prepared for the freeze over when he comes home tonight.

That is what I'm trying to say ... it's easy to love and be filled with closeness for your husband when you're standing outside an operating theatre. It is easy to cling to God when you have nowhere else to turn to.

No landslide or rollercoaster is going to kick us into action on the mundane. Nobody is going to send me good wishes and prayers that I will get dinner made this evening. Nobody

CHAPTER 2: THE FAMILY

is going to ring the doorbell and offer to put the children to bed because I must be tired by now. Nobody is going to notice whether I do the mundane or not. To be quite honest, nobody cares.

Well, not quite nobody. Your spouse cares. Your children care (though they probably do not know that yet and won't for about another twenty years or so).

And God cares. Because you are his family, and family is the heart word of God.

It's all very well knowing that marriage and family are important, but when it gets down to the mundane and nitty-gritty aspects of family life, we stumble all too easily. Theory is no good without some practical ideas of something I can do today and now. Over twenty-six years of marriage, I have gleaned some wisdom, oftentimes from talks, books or people I admire, other times just things I came up with myself which I found worked well and so became part of my arsenal.

I was once giving a morning workshop to a group of young mothers on the topic of marriage. I had the idea of playing a sort of game with them. I got them to close their eyes for twenty seconds, which is a long enough time, and to think about their own marriages and where they thought any holes might be. Everybody has things which jump out as the most obvious flaws or shortcomings.

18 ... 19 ... 20 ... time up!

Without asking the girls to reveal their private thoughts, I said that I suspected that most of the thoughts they had had began with:

"HE should ..."

"I wish HE would ..."

"I'd love HIM to ..."

When I said that, every one of the girls nodded and laughed guiltily. This is exactly what I expected because it is the way I think too. This is where we must start. It is very, very easy to see the faults of the other. The more we know them, as in our spouse, the more obvious they are to us. What's not so easy to see is where I am going wrong. I bet not one of those mums thought to herself, "If only I was more patient, less petty …"

Not one of us will ever reach the point where we can say "Ah yes, I'm perfect now!" No human relationship ever reaches that point, either. We need to chip away, all the time. We need to struggle against our weaknesses, to try and build up our qualities. So too with marriage. Whether we are newlyweds, hot off the press and rocking, or whether we're floundering, or we are nice and comfortable, every one of our marriages can be better. As we have heard time and again, we can only improve ourselves. Funnily enough, a change in ourselves often precipitates the desired change in the other.

I asked the girls to close their eyes again, and this time to think of the one thing each one could do better, humbling as that may be to admit.

They found this exercise far more inspiring, and each of them went home with small and realistic resolutions.

Marriage is fragile, just like ourselves who are made of earthen vessels, easily broken when not protected. Just how small are the tiny fissures which can shatter the strongest of rocks from repeated freeze-thaw-freeze-thaw action. The damage is not noticeable when the fissures are microscopic, but when the rock shatters. … it is too late then.

Not one of us is perfect, not one of us has the perfect spouse. We are all struggling. Sometimes, when in a slightly over-dramatic mood, I wonder to myself *what if?* What if my husband died? What would be the things I would regret not having done for him? Believe me, the list is extensive. I think over all I am not too bad as wives go, but I know those are things that would play on my mind because time cannot be re-lived. I would be sorry for not making his life nicer in those tiny moments. They are always small, but small is important.

Then, of course, what if *I* died? What would my husband be sorry about? Not in a babyish "he'll be sorry then" way, but what would he regret he had not done a bit better? What are the would haves, could haves, should haves?

The imaginary 'list' I compiled for my husband in these macabre, if entertaining thoughts is a lot shorter than mine, but indeed there are a few small things since, after all, he is human. They do not bother me, but I know they would bother him if such a thing were to happen.

You know the phrase 'don't sweat the small stuff'. I have never really believed in that philosophy. But now I think differently about that phrase. Yes, sweat the small stuff because it is the small stuff that counts. Small stuff is what builds up love and security, both in marriage and in every other sort of relationship. We can live without the grandiose gestures of champagne and spring in Paris, but we cannot live without the small acts of thoughtfulness such as finding your car refilled with petrol because your spouse knows you don't like that task, or always knowing that, hail or snow, your spouse will wave you off from the doorstep each morning and greet you with a smile that evening.

Sweat the small stuff … love the small stuff … because usually that is all we have to offer.

Rosa Pich

Rosa Pich and Josemaría Postigo, who sadly died in 2017, are the parents of a large family living in Barcelona. Rosa is the author of a book called *ROSA, What's your Secret?*

Josemaría and Rosa were both children of large families. Rosa worked part-time outside the home. In 2015, they received the European Large Family of the Year Award.

Rosa participated in various seminars about the family and appeared on television programmes around the world.

They are well-equipped to pass on their experiences about what a family is and about the rearing of children, especially in the society of the 21st century. Of course, all can be applied to families with any number of children.

Her book is divided in chapters, which has an illustration that deals with the topic in question. I picked up some of these at random, even though all would be relevant.

Family Meal

"Dinner is the occasion for the most important encounter of the day. It is the time when all members of the family can talk about their experiences and share personal anecdotes in a warm and pleasant environment.

Each family must discover which meal is their main one. Some parents get home late at night and make breakfast their daily family encounter. On holidays, it is usually lunch, whereas during the school year, dinner can be the best time. Meals in large families are often simple because life doesn't allow more to parents like us who work outside the home. But adding a touch of joy through decoration can make the family encounter more appealing.

The TV is not invited to such an important family gathering. We leave it in the sitting room, tucked away and out of sight. That way it doesn't interrupt our bustling, and often funny conversations."

Choice of School

"This is an important decision for any family – the choice of pre-school and a childcare provider for your children.

Parents must get involved in school and go to meetings, and learn how to bring kids up because we are not born knowing what to do here."

Work and Study

"As parents, we have the responsibility to know the real abilities of each child, not the ones we wish they had. We may have an artist at home, or a chef, or a future expert computer scientist. It is true that if they have the ability for it, we must encourage children to keep studying. For some, a single major is not enough, and they must pursue a double so as not to waste time. For others, achieving a single professional degree is sufficient."

Mom first, Dad first

"Communication in marriage is essential. You must say things to each other, but you have to do it at the right time and in the right tone. Yes, let's talk about forgiveness. In most cases what happens is a misunderstanding, but if we have failed at some point, we must ask each other for forgiveness, and forget about it. One who forgives and forgets is freer."

Speaking with the children ... being friends

"We must be willing to speak with our children all the time, to listen to them, to allow them to tell us whatever they need, even if we are tired and it's eleven at night. So many of them seem to come to the living room to read, and there is always one or two who want to talk about the latest news that has come into their heads. Your children must trust you."

Rosa has a chapter in the book about discipline, authority, etc. where she reminds parents that they are the first educators and must look at all aspects of their children's lives.

What I found striking was how many times the word 'NO' was written with capital letters, to emphasise the importance of not going along with everything the children suggest, and the relevance of educating a child in freedom and responsibility. These virtues are key for the future development of each child and the lasting impact it will make on their lives.

It is said that parents should have a certain respect for their children's freedom, according of course to their age. One can say that freedom and authority go hand-in-hand, and that if the answer to a request which is not suitable or convenient is 'NO', the best way forward is to get them to come to the same conclusion themselves, without having to actually pronounce the word.

CHAPTER 2: THE FAMILY

I understand that it is easier said than done, and that often in life we need to be able to say, even to adults, that their proposed way of acting is not appropriate if the request goes against the moral principles, which never change.

The Cremades Family

I came across a delightful story of another large family, the Cremades from Zaragoza. It is told by Javier Cremades, a priest of Opus Dei, now deceased (in March 2020). He entitles his book *Los planes de los Cremades* (The Cremades's Plans). It was published in Spanish in 2016.

The following are some of the experiences they had as a family and that are recounted in the book.

On 5th March 1964, the family decided that the best way to celebrate their 25th wedding anniversary was to go to Rome with the whole family and have an audience with the Holy Father, Paul VI. They planned also to meet the founder of Opus Dei, St Josemaría, while in Rome. On the first day, they went to St. Josemaría's house. He celebrated Mass for them in his own oratory and gave them a very encouraging homily, in which he remembered the days when he used to go to the poorer areas of Zaragoza to teach catechism with Javier's father, the children's grandfather.

After this they had a splendid breakfast with the founder. The children devoured the food quickly, helped by St. Josemaría who encouraged them. However, the parents were quite shocked at their children's manners.

Shortly after that, they went to the Vatican to meet the Holy Father.

All the young ones enjoyed the Swiss Guards, mimicking them, and prompting them to salute, which they did as if they were greeting important visitors. The parents observed all this behaviour and were trying to call them to order. The Holy Father was very affectionate with each one of them. The older ones told him they were in Opus Dei and that they prayed for him daily. He commented that "Opus Dei is a blessing from heaven." They got some photographs taken with him, and he also gave each rosary beads.

It was a great day, even though the parents had to reprimand the children for their behaviour.

St. Josemaría again invited them for 'merienda' (afternoon tea). Their mother warned them to eat well at lunch time, so as not to have a repetition of the previous episode, but it seemed not to register with them. When they arrived, The Father (the founder) sent a message to say he was delayed and to go ahead with the merienda. When he turned up the plates with the goodies were empty! They had eaten everything! The Father was delighted and ordered more food to be brought to them.

Javier doesn't tell in his story about the aftermath at home after this second experience. My guess is that when the parents were alone, they had a good laugh, and put aside the whole thing as anecdotal. There would be other opportunities in the future to teach them the proper way of behaving in a given situation.

CHAPTER 2: THE FAMILY

The Cremades family with St. Josemaría

A few words about the grandparents and the elderly

The contribution of the grandparents and the elderly to the wellbeing of the family is invaluable. They can help in so many practical ways, bringing the children to school, minding them at home when parents are out working, listening to their stories, guiding them to a greater knowledge of life.

St. John Paul II in the book *The Family Domestic Church* (Papal addresses on the Christian Family), mentions that:

"The elderly person must constitute for adults and young people a sure reference point in times of uncertainty, an incentive to live the higher values of the spirit, which never grow old and are still a precious link between the past generations and the present ones. This requires, however, that he be considered for what he gives now, but also for what he has given; not so much for what he does, but above all for what he is: it is necessary in a word, that the rich treasure of experience and wisdom, of which he is the bearer, be recognised and appreciated."

Sometimes the conditions for integrating grandparents into the family do not exist and the advice from the doctors 'you are not going to be able to look after him/her at home,' has to be carefully considered. Some families have had to have recourse to a nursing home to look after these loved ones. But the bond can still exist, and the responsibility to look after them with the utmost love and affection is still there.

The resources and imagination of families to make the stay of their loved ones in these institutions more bearable, even pleasant, are truly amazing. A friend of mine told me about her sister who is in one of those residences. Her sister loved birds and used to feed them in a corner of the garden at home, so when she went there, the birds gathered around the area. The sister decided to buy a bird cage which she installed outside the window of her room in the nursing home and keep it full of seeds. She now has the entertainment of watching the birds, lots of them, playing and feeding outside her window.

Dr. Miriam Kennedy

Dr. Miriam Kennedy, Consultant Psychiatrist and Clinical Director in Highfield Healthcare in Dublin, explains in an article published in the *Irish Times Health Supplement*, what a nursing home meant to their family:

"A nursing home is not a hospital, it is not a residence, it is an extension of your own family home.

The decision to bring my mother to a nursing home came after many years of illness and efforts on the part of my sister and me to look after two parents with multiple illnesses. My father was in hospital due to physical problems, multiple heart attacks, seizures, etc. My mother had developed symptoms which we later found were part and parcel of a state of dementia.

Before this, the one weekend myself and my sister happened to leave the country – the only time we were both away at the same time in years – my elderly father woke up in the night to find my mother had got out of the bed and had fallen against the sink in the corner of the room, splitting her skull wide open.

He, with multiple heart attacks, followed the ambulance that brought her to the hospital. How he didn't have another heart attack that night was amazing. This seemed to be a turning point: the image of her falling, her vulnerability and the bleeding, did not leave him and led to the decision which we had all been avoiding for a long time.

It had come to the point when our multiple attempts of providing full-time care, and our many efforts to get additional home help, were failing more and more. The strain on my father was evident and the worry that Mum was not being helped as she needed it, grew. He wanted to look after her himself. After all, in marrying her, he had gone against his particular background, Catholic rural Ireland, in marrying a beauty queen, who was musical, romantic and artistic, from a family of immigrant orthodox Jews. The life they forged together was one that he was deeply at one with. He wanted to protect her forever. Eventually, a very kind geriatrician said to us "Your mother needs 24-hour physical care to attend to her everyday needs." And so, because it was better for her, as outlined by the geriatrician, the decision was made that she would go to a nursing home.

After a lot of research, we finally found a nursing home where the woman in charge had a personality which was kind, engaged, loving and human towards the people who were entrusted to her care.

We had spent time explaining to all the teams involved about Mum's tendency to panic, thus the timely and orderly transfer to the nursing home was important. Her understanding was that she would go to this place for further rest and help. But how much she took in, I don't know.

For different reasons, there was a long delay, and when we arrived at the nursing home, she was met by the night shift and by somebody who we later heard was there as a stand-in for a week. Before we knew it, she was bundled upstairs, out of her clothes, and into her nightdress. All this terrified her. She started to scream and became agitated. I insisted on

CHAPTER 2: THE FAMILY

going into the room. The hospital had told us she could have a sedative and an injection which they gave her.

My sister and myself were beside ourselves, feeling helpless and very sad, not knowing what to do. Our father had just come out of coronary care after yet another heart attack. We had hoped to save him the worry having told him how nice the place was, how welcoming the staff were and how they were prepared for her. I said to my sister, "There is nothing else for it, I am going to get Dad."

I went and got my father, complete with his recently inserted pacemaker, and he came up the stairs, coughing, to the top room where Mum was in a distressed state. He went over to her, all six feet of him, and calmly and lovingly kissed her on the lips. With that, she became completely tranquil. He placed her head back gently on her pillow, pulled up the sheets, tucked them under her chin, kissed her on the forehead, and said, "Now don't worry, sleep, rest and I will be here in the morning."

She slept right through the night.

Amazed at how quickly this had worked, and how beautifully intimate that moment was, I thought about how my parents were very united, and yet not normally given to external shows of affection. This tender kiss was a special moment between the two. Later on, I asked Dad, "How did you do that?" His answer was a big smile, that characteristic humorous smile, that typifies many men from the same county (Kerry):

"Years of practice, years of practice," he replied.

I drove him home and he also slept soundly. He then proceeded to visit her day by day, for hours, and she always knew him and enjoyed his company. They remained deeply connected until the day he died before Mum some years later.

The care she received in the nursing home was outstanding, but more important were the details and affection that surrounded her. When she died, the nurses and carers were crying as much as we were."

During the pandemic, we witnessed the care the nursing homes give to our elderly citizens and heard many stories showing the beautiful relationship between the young and the elderly, between grandparents and grandchildren.

Pope Francis wrote a letter to grandparents and the elderly. From now on, July 25th feast day of Ss Joachim and Anne (the grandparents of Jesus), will be dedicated as a day to commemorate the elderly and grandparents.

I thought it would be appropriate to insert here a few of his words which are comforting:

"I want to tell you that you are needed in order to help build the world of tomorrow, the world in which we together with our children and grandchildren will live, in a spirit of fraternity, once the storm has subsided. [Here, he is referring to the pandemic, currently affecting the world.]

"All of us must take an active part in renewing and supporting our troubled societies. Among the pillars that supports this new edifice, there are three that you can help to set up. Those three pillars are dreams, memories and prayer. The Lord's closeness will grant to all, even the frailest among us, the strength needed to embark along the path of dreams, memories and prayer. (...) The future of the world depends on this covenant between young and old. Who if not the young can take the dreams of the elderly and make them come true? Yet for this to happen, it is necessary that we continue to dream. Our dreams of justice, peace, solidarity can make it possible for young people to have new visions. In

this way, together we can build the future."

Before I finish this chapter on the family, I would like to mention couples that have received with joy, and indeed sometimes with trepidation, the addition to their home of a disabled child. The family has a great role to play in the integration of the disabled child at home and in the life of society. It has been noticed and sometimes it has come to light through individual stories about these people, that the way they are happier and more at ease is when these children are not seen as a burden to parents and siblings, when they are treated as just one more family member. When there is love, the difficulties disappear as some of the following stories will show.

The following is from the Vatican Conference: Integration of the Disabled (1999):

"The loving acceptance and care which the family can give to their mentally handicapped child, must aim at facilitating his future participation in the life of society. The document affirms as a basic principle, the fact that the disabled person is a 'fully human subject' endowed with a unique dignity as a human being. A disabled person's dignity, founded as it is on his nature as a human person desired by God, is neither diminished by the gravity of his handicap nor conditioned by his difficulty in communicating with others. This dignity cannot be rejected, nor can it be lost, no one's dignity can be taken away. It remains the same to the last moment of one's life."

Joseph Pearce in his book, *Race with the Devil,* tells us about his own son

On St. Patrick's Day 2002, our son Leo was born. He had Down's syndrome and would later be diagnosed as having autism. What a joy he has been over the past eleven years! What a joy and what a blessing!

Fr. Ho Lung of the Missionaries of the Poor describes those with Down's syndrome as 'by definition, love.' They live on love, and they live to love. They are basic elemental human nature, in all its beauty and simplicity. We know that if anyone has a Down's syndrome child, they can be sure that joy, laughter and love have been given to them as a special gift from God. There is no ambition, no battle for power, no pomp, no falsehood, no hypocrisy in Down's syndrome people. As Leo's father, I know from the beauty of experience that our son is a special gift from God. He has brought joy, laughter and love to our family, as well as challenges that are themselves gifts. It has been said that most of us are given life in order to learn, whereas a special few are given life in order to teach. How true this statement is! Leo has taught us so much! He has taught us to love more truly. He has taught us to give ourselves more fully. He has helped us to lay down our lives for those we love. Could he have given us a greater gift?"

The following are two stories from the magazine *Down Syndrome Ireland, More than Medical*

Aislinn and Paul

Aislinn and Paul, talk about their daughter Caoimbhe:

"Caoimbhe brings an extra dimension in life. Little things are big moments for her. She is full of love, affection and has a positive, simplistic outlook on life. (…) Caoimbhe has slotted right in and taught us things about ourselves that we didn't know."

Vanessa and David

Twenty minutes after Ceadaoin's birth, we received his Down's syndrome diagnosis. I screamed; David was dumbstruck. That lasted five minutes. We held him in our arms and the love was immediately overwhelming. The need to protect him and help him be the best he can be, was amazing. He is just our boy. Our family was instantly accepting and supportive. He was our new baby, a new grandson, a new nephew, a new cousin. We embrace this new chapter in our life.

Adam King

Most people in Ireland – courtesy of *The Late Late Show* – know Adam King, the six-year-old boy, who was brought to the Toy Show in November 2020 by Ryan Tubridy. His story made headlines not only in Ireland, but all over the world.

Adam was born with osteogenesis imperfecta type 2,

which causes brittle bones.

Adam has a dream of commanding a space mission with NASA one day. When he was asked if he would like to be an astronaut, he said calmly: "I can't be an astronaut because I have brittle bones." So it is a dream. Among his admirers was the global space community. A Tweet was placed on social media from NASA: "Adam's kind heart and adventurous spirit inspires us at NASA, and we can't wait for him to one day join our team of dreamers. We'll be here when he is ready."

His father David explains the surprise of the family and their appreciation of the reaction Adam provoked. "We have been absolutely blown away by everything that happened this weekend, and as a family we are very humbled and very grateful. It made me realise that people are good, they are good locally and globally. What was wonderful to us was that so many people were getting to see what we have seen in Adam since the day he was born. We have always known how spirited he is, and it was lovely to see that coming across on the show."

Adam is lucky to have a family that looks after him so well and that are proud of him and love him so much.

Everything within family life, its history, its traditions, etc. is a help to the development of its members. Every family has its own personality as we have seen in the stories above. Perhaps it is within this atmosphere that we can appreciate the value of little things, the ordinary things: 'small is beautiful.' So many details which help to make life pleasant and at times more bearable for everyone.

CHAPTER 2: THE FAMILY

Adam King with his parents

Adam King

"Friendship has an incalculable social value, since it fosters harmony among family members, and the creation of social environments more worthy of the human person. (…) This environment of friendship, which each of us is called to carry with us, is the fruit of many efforts to make life pleasant for others. Growing in cordiality, joyfulness, optimism, refinement and in all virtues that make living with others agreeable, is important for helping people to feel welcomed and to be happy: "A pleasant voice multiplies friends, and a gracious tongue multiplies courtesies." (Sir 6:5)."

Mgr. Fernando Ocariz, Prelate of Opus Dei,

Letter, Nov. 2019 no. 9.

CHAPTER 3

FRIENDSHIPS

A lot has been written and said about friendship. If we were to ask a number of people about the topic, I am sure we could add many more original views and interesting ideas to what already has been written or said. Or they might tell you – and this is probably more likely – that they can't explain it, but they can see it in action in their own environment, or that they themselves have had a living experience of what it is to have good friends, to maintain good friendships. Sometimes it has been called a 'very noble thing'.

I think there is something mysterious about friendship, and perhaps this is the reason why it is difficult to explain.

Man is a social being. We were not created to be on our own. Social interaction is a necessity of our nature. It is not surprising that in this process we find someone we can be friends with, not because we have the same temperament, or like the same things, or live in the same city, or work in the same place, but simply because we seem to get on. 'I am at home with this person, he/she understands me.'

The following are some of the ideas that come to mind when thinking about friendship.

The ability to be a good communicator and a good listener is part of what it means to be a good friend. Being able to understand where people are coming from and being interested in what they are telling us. And perhaps managing to bring another light to some issue and explaining why we hold a different view on that topic. Friendship is tested when opposite views come into play and we realise we need to broaden our understanding of different viewpoints.

We also need to cultivate patience because it can happen that we are being told 'that story' again, even though we may have heard it many times before from the same person. We could approach this situation as we might, for instance, if someone were to ask us something like 'Would you like to hear Beethoven's Violin Concerto?' We may have valid reasons for not listening to it at that moment, but we would never say, 'No thanks, I have already heard it.'

Naturalness and simplicity are good qualities to bring to a

friendship: the ability to be exactly as one is and not wanting to appear what one is not. This simplicity can also apply to the way in which we have dialogue with others. If we are trying to convince someone about something we consider is important for their own good, the simple way with some examples is perhaps the more likely to achieve good results. Once a friend of mine told me that she was trying to encourage her husband to go to the sacrament of confession. She went herself regularly, and it gave her such peace that she thought she would like to share this with her husband. There was no way to convince him, however.

One day, he accompanied her to the church where she was going to confession and sat in the queue waiting for her. He was seated a few rows in front of her. At one stage she noticed that a lady who was sitting beside him was talking to him and to her amazement she saw her husband get up and go straight into the confessional. It transpired that the lady had simply said to him 'You are next.'

I understand that it doesn't always work like that, but you never know. There is also the power of grace working in the soul, as is evident in this case.

I also remember a conversation I had with a friend, who was a Co-operator of Opus Dei during a retreat she was doing in our conference centre in Ireland. She loved the Work and helped in whatever way she could. So much so that I thought perhaps she would like to ask for admission as a supernumerary. Her answer was a very definite NO. Looking at a photograph of Aunt Carmen – as we call her in Opus Dei, the founder's sister – placed on the table in front of us, she said to me: "She was never in Opus Dei."

This lady was right. God has his own ways!

Aunt Carmen certainly received a mission which she followed with a generosity without bounds. She could have had a very comfortable position in life, but instead gave up her independence and put her whole heart into the service of Opus Dei. She turned down proposals of marriage in order to be available to what was needed from her. And she did it with generosity and willingness, and also with good humour! Those who knew her really loved her and were considered very lucky to have met her. She, together with her mother, helped to shape the family atmosphere presently in the Work, for which we are very grateful.

She could tell us a lot about friendship with her generosity and self-giving.

This ability to be natural and straightforward in our conversations will help us avoid disagreements and create a calm atmosphere even when we are dealing with topics that could create tension. This can also apply to the way in which we judge situations and events. It is helpful here to avoid drama and exaggeration. It seems that artists say they don't *finish* their paintings, they just *leave* them. Maybe that motto can help us, too, in certain situations with different people. A sense of humour can help greatly also.

Bishop Barron in his podcasts and conversations offers some helpful hints to bear in mind on the subject of friendship and social communication. Some points that he makes are:

"Every person is worthy of respect.

Be careful of the two options in an argument: violently imposing, or bland tolerance.

CHAPTER 3: FRIENDSHIP

Try to find some common ground.

Seek to persuade, not antagonise, to win the other person. Am I pursuing the truth or am I trying to win the argument?

Proposing, not imposing

Good to have a 'referee' in an intellectual conversation."

We are living in society which may surprise us in its approach to certain issues. For example, accepting things too readily without questioning their suitability and correct moral orientation. Sometimes, it seems that what really matters is what you think, or how you *feel* about something, instead of the reality and the truth of the thing itself. Certain situations in life will require that we try to clarify the ideas and help change the behaviour of someone who is wrong. We need to do this, especially in our friendships.

We may be familiar with the phrase often found in the novels of Jane Austen and other similar classics of the time: "Come and take tea with us." There is no better way to get to know someone than having a meal together, or a cup of coffee or tea. This can be one of the ways where friendships grow and become strengthened.

The whole subject of service is an interesting one, and very important when talking about friendships. Saint Josemaría used a lovely phrase: "We need to be a carpet so that others can tread softly." It tells a whole story.

In reality, in many of the activities we are engaged in, our work, our relationships with others in our family and social life, whether we realise it or not, we serve, we do something for the benefit of others. Yes, we work because it provides us with the means to maintain a family, to pay our own expenses, to live up to certain standards. But we can also achieve higher goals by making use of the opportunities offered us to become more aware of those around us, or their needs. This may require a change in our mentality and intention. To serve others does not mean just giving material things, money, or engaging in humanitarian work. Service also means trying to foster a better relationship, learning to respect and understand people, and meeting them on their level.

To serve sometimes means that we have to forgo our plans to help someone in need. To do something unpleasant, to smile when we are provoked or challenged. To take care of our body language.

Saint Josemaría Escrivá in his book *Friends of God (n. 173)* speaks about charity as something that *"moves us to respond differently to different people, adapting ourselves to their specific circumstances so as to give joy to those who are sad, knowledge to those who lack it, affection to the lonely."*

It is commonly understood that about 60% of our communication is shown through our body language. How often have we misunderstood someone because of their facial expressions, or a gesture of discontent, or some other sign which expressed something not intended by the person? On the other hand, sometimes because of charity, good manners or deference, we may have to pretend something contrary to what we feel.

I can't recall where I found the following interpretation of body language:

"Body language can also be used as a mask to convey contrary feelings. How often you have nodded firmly when you did not understand

CHAPTER 3: FRIENDSHIP

one word, smiled when your instinct was to scowl, clapped enthusiastically at the end of a talk that nearly put you to sleep. That doesn't mean you should go around with a fixed smile on your face. In these cases, you were not being hypocritical, but using body language positively as a mechanism of good manners."

The power of silence. It can also play a big part in our relationships. How many times we have regretted having said something, realising too late that we should have kept quiet and let things go. Silence is part of our non-verbal communication, and has been acknowledged as a powerful tool in the area of communication, especially in family relationships and relationships at work. Think of the phrase 'silence is golden'. There are many times when it becomes clear that it is better to say nothing in our conversations, where 'silence speaks, when words cannot'. I understand silence is often used as an effective tool in interviews, to evaluate the skills of the prospective candidate for the job.

Phillipa Foot, an English Philosopher (1920-2010) and one of the founders of contemporary virtue ethics, said in an interview with Harvard University that she was very interested in what she found in the second part of the Summa Theologica of St. Thomas where he speaks about virtues and vices, quoting St. Augustine. Phillipa Foot comments that "St. Augustine calls loquaciousness a vice, if indeed it is a vice. I put the question to a student of mine: *'Why on earth should loquaciousness be a vice?' And the answer was that if one is always talking, one doesn't have time to think. I was very interested in this, it seemed to be right."*

History has provided us with examples of the most unlikely – humanly speaking – friendships.

The friendship between J.K. Chesterton and George Bernard Shaw was published in *Mercator Net c/-New Media Foundation* by Karl Schmule, founding member of Campion in Sydney.

G.K.Chesterton/George Bernard Shaw

Chesterton won praise for his lifelong friendships with public figures whose views he opposed. Perhaps the most notable was George Bernard Shaw.

'I have argued with him,' said Chesterton, 'on almost every subject in the world: and have always been on opposite sides, without affectation or animosity. It is necessary to disagree with him as much as I do, in order to admire him as I do; and I am proud of him as a foe even more than as a friend.'

"Chesterton defended such causes as natural family, the independence of private property, and a patriotic love of one's nation, against Shaw's preferences for the power of the State, international government and the evolution of a superior humanity. Throughout endless disagreements, they remained devoted friends. Chesterton praised Shaw for his 'fairmindedness and intellectual geniality' while Shaw, who was personally wealthy, gave practical help by sponsoring public debates when Chesterton was financially strapped."

Pope Paul II/Gilbert Levine

The following is the amazing story of the friendship between St. John Paul II and Gilbert Levine, the Jewish American

CHAPTER 3: FRIENDSHIP

Director of the Kraków Orchestra Philharmonic.

Gilbert's grandparents on his father side, had emigrated to America from Poland. His wife Vera was from Bratislava. Her mother survived the Holocaust, even though many aunts, uncles, nieces and nephews had died in Auschwitz, Birkenau.

In 1987, Gilbert was invited to go to Kraków to conduct the Philharmonic orchestra. At the request of his mother-in-law, he promised to go to Auschwitz. That visit made a huge impact on him and also on his musical performances later on. On that occasion, shortly before leaving Kraków, he was offered the position as Director of the Orchestra. After considering the various challenges and difficulties involved, and speaking about it to his family, he decided to accept the offer.

Shortly after taking the job, the Archbishop of Kraków sent him a message to say that the Pope would like to receive him the following day. He was told to contact Monsignor Stanislaw Dziwisz, the Pope's secretary, to make all necessary arrangements, and also to bring his wife with him. They managed to sort out the business of arranging the journey at such a short notice, and the first visit took place. At the conclusion of this visit, the Pope said to him: "Maestro, I will see you at your concert." Gilbert did not know what that meant, but it transpired that the Pope wanted him to conduct a concert to commemorate the tenth anniversary of His Holiness Pontificate in the Vatican the following December. This was the beginning of a series of concerts he performed in the Vatican. He became known as the Pope's *Maestro*. It was also the beginning of a friendship that would last for many years until the Pope's death in 2005.

Gilbert Levine and his family with Pope St John Paul II in Rome in 2004

In an interview that took place in 2014, Gilbert spoke about this friendship.

"The relationship deepened through concerts, conversations and my art; he took my language, music, and used it for his own purposes."

This friendship between Gilbert and the Pope extended to his family, including his mother-in-law, the survivor of the Holocaust, with whom he had long conversations. The Pope

CHAPTER 3: FRIENDSHIP

was very appreciative of the work that Gilbert was doing, and on one occasion he said to him:

"Thank you so much for going to Kraków and thank you for bringing Kraków to me."

In one of his visits, Gilbert told the Pope he would like to organise a concert in Rome to commemorate the Shoah, and that he would like his Holiness to attend. The Pope immediately expressed his wish to make this concert a 'Papal Concert' – it would become a Vatican event. It would take place in the *Sala Nervi* in the Vatican with the orchestra from Rome and the choir from Kraków .

It was a time in which there were no relations between Israel and the Holy See, and when relationships between Catholics and Jews were strained. But in spite of the opposition he encountered within the Jewish Community, Gilbert commented that "the concert to commemorate the Shoah was one of the hardest creative challenges I ever undertook." It was an amazing success, attended by the Pope, the President of Italy, and the Chief Rabbi, all seated on an equal level.

One hundred and fifty survivors of the Holocaust were also present. They had met the Pope in a private audience in the *Sala Clementina* in the Vatican the morning before the concert. The Pope spoke to each one of them, and in his speech, he talked about "the unbreakable bond between Christians and Jews and he quoted the last verse of the very Psalm we would perform in Bernstein's setting that evening. How good and how pleasant it is when brothers live together in unity."

The concert surpassed their expectations. It became clear that music was the way of reaching out to others, it was a celebration of peace through music. "We had found the language that makes the worlds come together," Gilbert said. Of course, the Ninth Symphony of Beethoven was played, and he comments: "This had to be the Beethoven Ninth of a lifetime. I like to imagine Beethoven, who was always a son of the Church, smiling down on us, proud of the distinguished part his music had played in our common spiritual journey that night."

After 9/11, the Pope decided to host another concert of reconciliation, again in the Vatican. This was to promote reconciliation among believers in Islam, Judaism and Christianity. It was the last concert Saint John Paul II attended.

When asked in an interview what it was like to have known a saint, Gilbert commented: "He shared my Jewish faith and respected the fact that I was a faithful Jew. Through my association with the Pope, music and spirit became one and he saw music as a way of conveying universal ideas."

The book *The Pope's Maestro* tells in great detail the whole story: "This is a compelling tale of faith, friendship, and the healing power of music, to bring people together." (Amazon Review)

As we have already seen in the chapter on the Workplace, fostering culture forms part of our way of living. We could say the same about music. In it we can find a common language.

CHAPTER 3: FRIENDSHIP

Jackie Kennedy/Irish Priest Fr. Leonard

Recently, with the help of the *Irish Times*, I found and read about the story of Jackie Kennedy and her friendship with an Irish priest, Fr. Joseph Leonard, which she maintained for many years, from 1950 until his death in 1964. He was like a father figure to Jackie. She wrote to him regularly, and in her letters, she poured her heart out to him, and acknowledged the crucial importance of their correspondence. "It is so good to write all this down and get it off your chest because I never really talk to anyone." The letters he sent her confirm their close friendship and his role as a spiritual confidante.

In her early letters she wrote: "I suddenly realized this Christmas when my sister and I decided – after not going to church for a year – that we desperately wanted to change and get close to God again – that it must have been your little prayers that worked, all the way across the ocean."

And in another early letter: "I really want to be a good Catholic now and I know it is all because of you. I suppose I realized in the back of my mind you wanted that. You gave me the rosary beads as I left Ireland."

After her husband was elected President, she wrote: "We think of you often and wish we could have sent a magic ship to bring you over and spend some time in the sun with us. With our loves and our hopes that you will continue to pray for us."

Fr. Leonard replied that he wished Jackie and the President every grace and blessing for the year and many other years to come and thanked her for a beautiful book she sent about the White House. "With love to you both, I am as I have ever been, your devoted and affectionate friend."

Jackie Kennedy with Fr. Leonard in Ireland

The JFK Library archives contain another letter handwritten by Fr. Leonard, the day after Jackie's new-born baby died: "My dearest Jackie, I hope yourself and the President will allow me to join in your grief at the death of your little son who is enjoying the glories of eternal life."

As everyone knows, her husband J.F. Kennedy was murdered in her presence in November 1963. During the days after the assassination, she was shattered and bewildered to the point of asking God to take her life. Her brother-in-law, Bobby Kennedy, advised her to speak to a priest. In a letter written to Fr. Leonard after the assassination, she revealed how the tragedy left her struggling with her Catholic faith. "I am so bitter against God, but only He and you and I know that. Was God in the bullet that killed Jack? I do not want to be bitter or bring up my children in a bitter way. I am trying to make my peace with God, or I have no hope." Later, in the same letter, "God will have a bit of explaining to do to me if I ever meet him." She asked Fr. Leonard to pray for her and said she would pray too in order to overcome her bitterness against God. "I have to think there is a God or I have no hope of finding Jack again."

Gabriela from Valencia

The following is the story of Gabriela. She works in a dress designer shop in Valencia and, through the medium of TV, found a 'friend' who radically changed her life. She is married and has three children. The title of her story, which appeared on YouTube, is: *TV changed my life.*

She had been far from the faith for many years, but "I met God while zapping during Holy Week."

She tells us that when she was thirteen years of age, she abandoned all Christian education she had received at home and at school.

"I abandoned it for convenience, and I stopped practising my faith. I was a problematic teenager. My parents were such saints, and so were my brothers and sisters. I no longer went to Mass, and I spent my time doing very little and trying to enjoy myself a lot. In reality, I think I never lost my faith completely. My mother was always telling me: "Gabriela, if you don't take care of your faith, you will lose it." But I know I was leaving God up there far away in heaven, and didn't want to look at him, so that I could do what I wanted to do.

I got married when I was twenty-three, having met my husband four months previously, and I was madly in love with him. My lifestyle continued to be frivolous and superficial. We had a family. When my daughter was preparing for her Holy Communion, I was following all this preparation at a distance. I vaguely thought I had to do something about my spiritual life. I consulted some books in the hope that I might find some answers to my questions on my spiritual life.

And here is where television enters. It was Easter and Mel Gibson's newly released film *The Passion* was advertised. Someone asked me would I like to see it. My answer was a definite 'no'. Shortly after that, I was alone at home and sitting on the couch and before I knew it, I was looking at the Passion of the Christ.

CHAPTER 3: FRIENDSHIP

While looking at it, everything changed for me. I realised suddenly the Lord loves me. I felt as if he was saying 'Hey Gabriela, here I am,' and immediately I said to myself: 'Gabriela you believe in God who is not just in heaven anymore. This is Jesus Christ who has redeemed you and loves you even though you have turned away from him since you were thirteen years.'

I went to confession shortly after that and decided I would return to Mass on Sunday. The following Sunday was Palm Sunday and while there I felt an enormous joy. I am coming home! I could not stop crying. I was very moved.

All the time after this, I was looking forward to going to Mass on Sundays so that I could be with Him. But I kept thinking that surely there must be something else I can do for the Lord besides the Sunday Mass.

And here again television came to my rescue. While watching a programme about the Muslim world, I was impressed by the way they lived their faith: they made trips to Mecca, they lived Ramadan, had times of prayer. I thought to myself if Muslims have these practices, surely Christians must have something similar?

Then I remembered that my mother had given me from time to time, books, leaflets, the Gospels, etc. which I had carefully put in a shoe box and stored away in a drawer in my room. I found the gospels and for some reason I began at a page entitled *The day of a good Christian*. There I learned about the morning offering, the work of the day, the Angelus. I found it impossible not to fall in love with Jesus while reading the gospels. It was like a tornado or tsunami for me. I wanted to know everything at once, my faith, the church, the liturgy…

A really good example for me was my mother who has been a supernumerary member of Opus Dei since I was a little child. My mother is a wonderful, coherent woman who lives her life and faith at a high level without preaching. She always supported me and showed me examples of faith and understanding through her behaviour and affection.

I am so grateful now to be aware of the love of Our Lord. I have been enjoying this great gift in the last few years and trying to pass it on to other people. Naturally, it involves a struggle, but it is so worthwhile."

The following story may not be entirely related to friendship, but it explains the fact that it was through friendship that Dong and his wife found their vocation to holiness and apostolate in Opus Dei through the example of and friendship with their fellow parishioners.

Dong Hinderer, business executive in Chicago

Interview which appeared on YouTube in 2007

"I was born in Illinois, Chicago, into a normal family with one brother and sister. I met my wife while I was a student and we got married sixteen months later. I have worked in different companies as a business executive.

When the children were born, we moved close to Chicago. There we met a couple in the local parish to which we were attached. They were wonderful people, very peaceful and never anxious about anything. They had five children. My

CHAPTER 3: FRIENDSHIP

wife wanted to meet this lady to discover her secret. 'Perhaps she drinks before coming to church.'

We became friendly with this couple and my wife was invited to a recollection which was given by a priest of Opus Dei. I actually attended one for men around the same time. When I heard the priest talking about sanctifying ordinary life right where you are, that any job you have can be a path to holiness, it was like being hit in the head with a boulder.

My wife started attending a doctrine class which was given by this lady. I was a bit sceptical at first as I had never heard of a lay person giving a doctrine class. And then one day my wife said that she wanted to join Opus Dei. I was totally surprised and began to question her decision. In the end, we both joined Opus Dei.

I love Opus Dei and would like everyone to love it, but this is obviously not going to happen. Recently in a conversation with a parish priest who had misgivings about Opus Dei, I told him about my life, how I say the rosary every day and spend fifteen minutes doing some spiritual reading. I also do some mental prayer daily. He began to say that what I was doing sounded like a very good idea.

We are a family you can find anywhere. If you were a fly in the wall, you wouldn't see any difference between us and any other family. I hope perhaps we are more cheerful, and get on well among ourselves, and that we take our faith seriously. I still lose my temper occasionally, and then explain what I was angry about. I have kids who don't do well in school, and other kids who love school."

In answer to the question about himself being a saint he replied: "No way! I am a long way from sainthood, but I am never too far from the confessional."

The following are two stories (interviews) of unlikely friends which appeared recently on the website of Opus Dei.

Léa and Marie-Maude

Léa and Marie-Maude* are colleagues in Montreal, Canada. They became friends little by little, despite having very different backgrounds, beliefs, and interests.

* Names have been changed for privacy

How did the two of you meet?

Marie-Maude: We met at work. Léa was my first new colleague after a year and a half of remote work on a team of three people.

What makes you unlikely friends?

Marie-Maude: Léa comes from a very different background to what I am used to. She is more reserved and introverted, which contrasts with my more extroverted personality. I was intimidated by her level and field of study. I consider people with this level of education to be above average and generally very intelligent.

Léa: We have very different personalities. Marie-Maude thrives on social interaction and is comfortable in large events, while I find crowds quite draining. She's fearless and adventurous. For instance, she is an intrepid driver, while I tend to be nervous behind the wheel. I'll never forget the first time I got in her car!

Marie-Maude (laughs): Frankly, working remotely full-time made it more difficult to get to know people. At first, our exchanges were pragmatic and work-focused, not social, so it seemed unlikely that we would become real friends.

What changed?

Léa: Marie-Maude taught me to become a more alert and savvy person in the workplace, to overcome my naivety and navigate tricky work relationships. She shared her experience and hard-won expertise without asking for anything in return.

Marie-Maude: Being the same age and having studied at the same university in related fields made it easier to connect. Our work environment was new to Léa, and as two young women trying to find our place in the professional world, I felt a duty to help her in what is sometimes a difficult professional context. I tried to reassure her by identifying red flags.

It's not always easy to ask for or offer help. How did you build that level of trust as new colleagues?

Léa: We laughed together a lot, we did a photoshoot to renew our professional network pictures, and we went thrift shopping after work. We didn't spend all our time having difficult, heavy conversations, and I think those conversations were made easier by the spontaneity of our questions and our mutual honesty. Because we respect and trust each other, no topics are taboo between us.

Can you tell us about a time when one of you helped the other?

Marie-Maude: Soon after Léa took up her post, I had to leave for four months due to illness. This was very difficult for me and I found it hard to accept. It meant that Léa had to take on a large part of my responsibilities at short notice, even though she had only just started her job in a corporate world where adaptation normally takes several months. When I told her the news of my departure, she not only supported me but said she would pray for me. I didn't know what to think of that at the time. Actually, I thought it was a bit strange.

Was it awkward?

Léa: Our life paths and beliefs are very different, but Marie-Maude was always extremely open. That surprised me at first. When I talked to her about my faith she seemed very interested in knowing more, in a very positive way.

Marie-Maude: By the time I returned to work, we had the chance to develop our relationship further. I was able to better understand the meaning of 'praying for me' and grasp the significance of her offer ... which then really touched me. Whatever you call it (positive vibes, daily affirmations, or prayer), the reality is that I came back to work stronger. I know that her prayer contributed to my healing. For me, this memory says a lot about Léa. I see her as an altruistic, fundamentally good person who is always ready to help the people around her.

Léa: When I was going through a rather difficult time, she talked to me about my 'little Jesus' [*p'tit Jésus*] which touched me a lot, precisely because she does not believe in him like I do.

What's the most important thing each of you has learned from the other?

Marie-Maude: Léa helped me realise the value of kindness

in interpersonal relationships. Her days are full of contact with people of very different ages and cultures. I am always impressed by her consideration for everyone.

Léa: For me, honesty. Marie-Maude gave me an example of honesty in friendship, exercised with courage and thoughtfulness. She has a gift for capturing people, understanding them, and encouraging them by placing herself in their shoes. I thank God for placing her in my life.

Keegan Chad and Trevor Mofokeng

Keagan Chad and Trevor Mofokeng are science students at Nelson Mandela University in Port Elizabeth, South Africa.

How did the two of you meet?

Trevor: I met Keagan on campus through a mutual friend after a class that we had together.

Keagan: That's right. After a lecture, I met up with the only person from university I knew at the time, and she was standing next to Trevor and some other people I now call friends. We all met up outside the building and we spoke for a couple minutes and that's when I first started speaking to Trevor.

Trevor: It was a small group of about five people. We had a light conversation ranging between several topics and at one point, I remember all of us shaking hands and announcing ourselves to be friends, a random promise that we have all kept to this day.

What makes you unlikely friends?

Keagan: Our races definitely make us unusual friends.

Trevor: Keagan is white, and I am black. Port Elizabeth is one part of South Africa where race isn't a huge factor of life, but it remains a lingering background factor in a university environment, and students tend to group themselves according to their own race for their own preferred reasons and Keagan and I just happened to defy that factor.

Keagan: I consider myself an atheist, while Trevor is Christian. I've personally learned a lot about religion from him, and he has introduced me to some religious acts, like fasting.

Do you often talk about your differences?

Trevor: We talk about everything. Discussions of our differences don't have a starting point: they slide themselves into other conversations. We don't set out to talk about our differences, and when those conversations happen, they tend to go on for a while and die out by lack of contribution or the start of another conversation.

Keegan: It's easy to talk about sensitive topics with Trevor because he doesn't get offended easily. Some people would see the questions I ask him about religion as an attack against their faith, but he attempts to answer them logically.

Can you tell us about a time you shared your convictions with Trevor?

Keegan: I remember an interesting conversation about self-defence, sin and revenge. We were having lunch with a couple of other friends. We agreed that self-defence would be

CHAPTER 3: FRIENDSHIP

acceptable in the case of an attack, to protect a loved one, but Trevor said that it would be wrong to seek revenge another day because that sort of revenge is sinful. My response was that my main motive would be to avenge my loved one's life because I do not owe anything to a higher power. Trevor explained the consequences of my actions in light of that sort of situation referring to sin, the after-life and the science behind it. We never resolved that difference because the conversation was interrupted.

Do you think your friendship has made you better people?

Keegan: Definitely. I've learned how to interact with new people which I used to struggle with a lot more.

Trevor: And Keagan has taught me some useful social skills and has broadened my knowledge on how to approach certain topics, and how to give advice about intimate things. I believe that this has made me a much better friend.

Interesting. Can you give an example of a skill you've learned from Keagan?

Trevor: As a scientist, I have a lot of atheist friends, including Keagan. One conversation with him has sort of become my point of reference for other conversations with atheist friends or people of other beliefs. We were chatting over a Discord call and he mentioned that some scientists or atheists have difficulty believing in a higher power because they fear a being superior to humans. They want to feel in control. That insight helped me to have productive conversations with others and to choose my words carefully to avoid offending others.

You clearly respect one another's viewpoints.

Keegan: Yes, we do. When we have conversations about religion, I tell my views and beliefs to which he responds with his own or acknowledges. While I have learned a lot about religion from him, I still hold true to my beliefs as an atheist.

Trevor: We get a lot of judgment from other people, so we've sort of created a judgment-free (or "light-hearted judgment only") environment in our friendship, which allows me to be completely at ease with him.

How?

Trevor: Keagan is a good listener and quite an easy person to open up to. He's a very open-minded and light-hearted guy, so conversations between us never sound too heavy. We also open up to each other about intimate or personal things, something a lot of young men do not do.

What advice would you give other young men who want to form deep friendships the way you two have?

Keagan: I would say that it's always easier to tell someone about what's making you anxious than continue to carry the weight on your shoulders alone. We often talk about what stresses we face in our lives, such as university work and we're quite open about personal experiences that would normally be difficult to talk about. A lot of the conversations offer a lot of relief.

Most of the stories on friendship also unfold and develop within the framework of ordinary life, of life within the family, in work situations, or while one is involved in hobbies or times of rest and relaxation. The value and worth of the small details underlying these relationships are very hard to measure because often they remain hidden in plain sight.

CONCLUSION

When thinking about a suitable conclusion for the book, I recalled a familiar phrase: 'Draw your own conclusions.' Obviously, there is room for more discussion, more insights, more understanding, more knowledge, in the matters dealt with. So, I thought that more than an actual conclusion, let everyone draw their own. I will call it a winding up with a consideration about a thought that may come to mind. *What is the purpose of my life?* which Pope Francis answers in *Gaudete et Exultate* n. 13: "Embrace that unique plan that God willed for each of us from eternity."

Peter Seewald in his book about Pope Benedict XVI, tells us that: *"At some point I had asked how many paths there were leading to God. The answer came back like a pistol. There were as many ways to God, he said, as there were people; since ultimately each person has his own path."* (*Benedict XVI, An Intimate Portrait*, Peter Seewald, p.227)

How do we go about finding that path?

In normal circumstances, as seen throughout the book, our lives evolve within a family, committed to professional work or an activity of some kind and most likely among friends. We can say that our paths are marked by various factors: our circumstances, the events that occur, our innate qualities, our dreams. As we are not dealing only with

CONCLUSION

scientific facts and figures, there is no guarantee that our choices will be the right ones. And here I will let St. Josemaría give us the answer, with words he repeated again and again throughout his life: "God speaks to us through everyday events and situations."

It is in this context we may discover God's call.

"It is very moving to think of so many Christian men and women who, perhaps without any specific resolve, are living simple, ordinary lives and trying to make them a living embodiment of the will of God. There is an urgent need in the Church to make these people conscious of the sublime value of their lives, to reveal to them that what they are doing, unimportant though it appears, has an eternal value." (St. Josemaría, Interview with the woman's magazine of the time, *Telva*).

Our happiness in this world lies mainly in finding the path God has traced for us. Then, both the positive and negative events and circumstances we encounter in this world, the ones that make us rejoice and the ones that make us suffer, will, as it were, blend into one: the will of God. And here is where we find the peace we seek.

We have been touching on important issues which greatly impact the lives of each one of us. There is a very good Podcast on the internet, *Hearts + Minds*, for "discussions on life, love, faith and everything else in between." They are very happy to chat about any topic.